WILTS

A GENEALOGICAL BIBLIOGRAPHY

— BY —
STUART A. RAYMOND

WILTSHIRE LIBRARY & MUSEUM SERVICE

FEDERATION OF FAMILY HISTORY SOCIETIES

Published by the
Federation of Family History Societies,
c/o The Benson Room, Birmingham & Midland Institute,
Margaret Street, Birmingham, B3 3BS, U.K.

Copies also available from:
S.A. & M.J. Raymond, 6 Russet Avenue, Exeter, Devon, EX1 3QB, U.K.

Copyright © S.A. Raymond, 1993

Text processed and printed by
Oxuniprint, Oxford University Press

Cataloguing in publication data:

RAYMOND, Stuart A., 1945- .
Wiltshire: a genealogical bibliography. British genealogical bibliographies.
Birmingham, England: Federation of Family History Societies, 1993.

DDC: 016.9291094231

ISBN: 1 872094 58 9

ISSN: 1033-2065

CONTENTS

INTRODUCTION

This bibliography is intended primarily for genealogists. It is, however, hoped that it will also prove useful to historians, librarians, archivists, research students, and anyone else interested in Wiltshire genealogy and local history. It is intended to be used in conjunction with my *English genealogy: an introductory bibliography*, and the other titles in the *British genealogical bibliographies* series. A full list of these titles is given on the back cover.

Many genealogists, when they begin their research, fail to realise just how much information is available in printed form. Not infrequently, they head straight for the archives, rather than checking printed sources first. The consequence is a considerable loss of time, and excessive use of irreplaceable archival materials. But, when faced with the vast array of tomes to be found in major libraries, it is difficult to know where to begin. This bibliography, in conjunction with the others in the series, is intended to help you find that beginning, and to provide guidance in following through the search for ancestors in printed sources. My aim has been to list everything of substance relating to Wiltshire that has been published, and is likely to be of use to genealogists. In general, I have not included works which are national in scope, but which contain Wiltshire material. Such works may be identified in *English genealogy: an introductory bibliography*. I have also excluded the numerous notes and queries found in such journals as *W.F.H.S.*, except where the content is of some substance. Where I have included such notes, replies to them are given in the form 'see also', with no reference to the names of respondents. Local and church histories are not included, except in a few cases. Such histories are frequently invaluable for genealogical purposes, but a full listing of them would require another volume. Newspaper articles are also omitted. This is a bibliography of published works; hence the many unpublished genealogical works to be found in libraries such as those at Trowbridge and Devizes are not listed here.

Be warned—I cannot claim that this bibliography is comprehensive. And total accuracy is, of course, impossible. I have physically examined most—but not all—of the items listed. Some works I have deliberately excluded; others I have undoubtedly missed. If you come across anything that has been missed, please let me know, so that it can be included in a second edition in due course.

Most works listed here are readily available in the libraries listed below—although no library holds everything. Even if you are overseas, you should be able to find copies of the more important works in larger research libraries. However, some items may prove difficult to locate. Never fear! Librarians believe in the principle that all publications should be universally available, and most public libraries are able to tap into the international inter-library loans network. Your local library should be able to borrow most of the items listed here, even if it has to go overseas to obtain them.

The work of compiling this bibliography has depended heavily on the libraries I have used. These included the British Library, Exeter University Library, Exeter City Library, the Somerset Archaeological and Natural History Society Library, the local studies library at Trowbridge, Wiltshire County Record Office, and Bristol University Library. I am grateful to the librarians of all these institutions for their help, and especially to Michael Marshman and Felicity Gilmour, of the Wiltshire Library & Museum Service, who both read the first draft of this book. I am also grateful to the Wiltshire Family History Society for their assistance—especially to Richard Moore who also read the first draft, and to Joyce and Jim Lanfear who not only arranged the loan of their journal, but also provided tea and companionship whilst I waited for the AA after I had locked my keys in the car! My thanks to Terry Humphries, who typed this book, to Jeremy Gibson, who has provided much needed encouragement, and to the officers of the Federation of Family History Societies, whose support is vital to the success of *British genealogical bibliographies*.

Stuart A. Raymond

LIBRARIES AND RECORD OFFICES

Wiltshire Library & Museum Service
Bythesea Road
TROWBRIDGE
Wilts., BA14 8BS

Wiltshire Record Office
Bythesea Road
TROWBRIDGE
Wilts., BA14 8JG

Wiltshire Archaeological & Natural History Society
41 Long Street
DEVIZES
Wilts., SN10 1NS

In addition, most branches of the Wiltshire County Library hold local studies material—especially at Devizes, Salisbury and Swindon.

BIBLIOGRAPHIC PRESENTATION

Authors' names are in SMALL CAPITALS. Book and journal titles are in *italics*. Articles appearing in journals and material, such as parish register transcripts, forming only part of books are in inverted commas and textface type. Volume numbers are in **bold** and the individual number of the journal may be shown in parentheses. These are normally followed by the place of publication (except where this is London, which is omitted), the name of the publisher and the date of publication. In the case of articles, further figures indicate page numbers.

ABBREVIATIONS

M.G.H.   *Miscellanea Genealogica et Heraldica*
N.S.   New Series
P.P.R.S.   *Phillimore's Parish Register Series*
W.A.M.   *Wiltshire Archaeological and Natural History Magazine*
W.F.H.S.   *Wiltshire Family History Society [Journal]*
W.N.Q.   *Wiltshire Notes & Queries*
W.P.R.M.   *Wiltshire Parish Registers: Marriages*
W.R.S.   Wiltshire Record Society

1. THE HISTORY OF WILTSHIRE

The purpose of genealogy is to know who your ancestors were, and to understand them. If you want to do this adequately, and to understand how they lived, worked, ate, slept and worshipped, then you need to read up on local history. For Wiltshire, a good beginning is provided by two works:

WATKIN, BRUCE. *A history of Wiltshire.* Chichester: Phillimore, 1989.
BETTEY, J.H. *Wessex from A.D. 1000.* Longman, 1986.

The authoritative work from the *Victoria County History* is:

PUGH, R.B., & CRITTALL, ELIZABETH, ET AL, eds. *A history of Wiltshire.* Oxford University Press for the Institute of Historical Research, 1955-91. 14 vols. Contents: v.1(1-2). Archaeology. v.2. Domesday book. v.5. Government. v.6. Wilton and Salisbury. v.7. Bradford Hundred; Melksham Hundred; Potterne and Cannings Hundred. v.8. Warminster Hundred; Westbury Hundred; Whorwellsdown Hundred. v.9. Kingsbridge Hundred. v.10. Swanborough Hundred. v.11. Downton Hundred; Elstub Hundred; Everleigh Hundred. v.12. Ramsbury Hundred; Selkley Hundred; Marlborough. v.13. Chalke Hundred; Dunworth Hundred. v.14. Malmesbury Hundred.

The earliest major work on Wiltshire history was compiled in the seventeenth century, although not actually published until 1862:

JACKSON, JOHN EDWARD. *Wiltshire: the topographical collections of John Aubrey, F.R.S., A.D. 1659-70 ... corrected and enlarged.* Devizes: Wiltshire Archaeological and Natural History Society, 1862. This is a parochial survey, with many genealogical notes, and pedigrees of Gore of Alderton, Snell of Kingston St.Michael, St.John of Lydiard Tregoze, Stradling, and Danvers of Dauntsey. See also:

AUBREY, JOHN. *Aubrey's natural history of Wiltshire.* Newton Abbot: David & Charles, 1969. Originally published Wiltshire Topographical Society, 1847. This includes a limited amount of genealogical information, and has a brief chapter on 'worthies'.

An important nineteenth century work, printing many charters, inquisitions post mortem, pleas, etc., and containing a parochial survey, is:

HOARE, SIR RICHARD COLT. *The modern history of South Wiltshire.* 6 vols. John Bowyer Nichols and John Gough Nichols, 1822-44. Alternative title: *The history of modern Wiltshire.* See also:

BRITTON, JOHN. *The beauties of Wiltshire displayed in statistical, historical and descriptive sketches ...* 3 vols. Vernon & Hood, et al, 1801-25. Includes lists of 'eminent persons', and of seats of noblemen and gentlemen, etc.

A more recent work, which includes much information of genealogical value, is:

CAMPION, P. *A recent history of Hampshire, Wiltshire, Dorset.* Poole: J. Looker, [1922].

A number of works provide information about Wiltshire seats and 'county' families:

BADENI, JUNE. *Wiltshire forefathers.* Malmesbury: privately printed, 1959. Gossipy book about North Wiltshire seats and families.

COOKE, ROBERT. *West country houses: an illustrated account of some country houses and their owners in the counties of Bristol, Gloucester, Somerset and Wiltshire ...* Bristol: R.Cooke, 1957. Includes notes on the descent of the houses described.

DELDERFIELD, E.R. *West country historic houses and their families, vol.2. Dorset, Wiltshire and North Somerset.* Newton Abbot: David & Charles, 1970.

ELYARD, S. JOAN. *Some old Wiltshire homes, with short notices on their architecture, history and associations.* Charles J. Cox, 1894.

Many scholarly books and articles on Wiltshire history have been written in recent years, and are worth reading—especially those based on sources used by genealogists. The following list is a very brief personal selection; it is arranged chronologically.

TAYLOR, C.C. 'Whiteparish: a study of the development of a forest-edge parish', *W.A.M.* **62**, 1967, 79-102. A landscape study.

NASH, A.E. 'The mortality pattern of the Wiltshire lords of the manor, 1242-1377', *Southern history* **2**, 1980, 31-43. Based on inquisitions post mortem.

HARE, J.N. 'The demesne lessees of fifteenth-century Wiltshire', *Agricultural history review* **29**, 1981, 1-15. Gives some names.

INGRAM, MARTIN. *Church courts, sex and marriage in England 1570-1640.* Cambridge: Cambridge U.P., 1988.

WALL, A.D. *Riot, bastardy and other social problems: the role of constables and J.P.'s, 1580-1625.* Trowbridge: Wiltshire Library Service, 1980.

The History of Wiltshire continued

SHARP, BUCHANAN. *In contempt of all authority: rural artisans and riot in the West of England, 1586-1660.* Berkeley: University of California Press, 1980. Mainly concerned with Gloucestershire and Wiltshire.

SLACK, PAUL. *Poverty and policy in Tudor and Stuart England.* Longman, 1988. Includes much information on Salisbury.

SLACK, P. 'Poverty and politics in Salisbury, 1597-1666', in CLARK, PETER, & SLACK, PAUL. *Crisis and order in English towns, 1500-1700: essays in urban history.* Routledge, 1972, 164-203.

TAYLOR, C.C. 'Population studies in 17th-century and 18th-century Wiltshire', *W.A.M.* **60**, 1965, 100-108.

UNDERDOWN, DAVID. *Revel, riot and rebellion: popular politics and culture in England, 1603-1660.* Oxford: Clarendon Press, 1985.

UNDERDOWN, D. 'The chalk and the cheese: contrasts among the English Clubmen', *Past and present* **83**, 1979, 25-48. A Civil War study.

JACKSON, S. 'Population change in the Somerset-Wiltshire border area, 1701-1800: a regional demographic study', *Southern history* **7**, 1985, 119-44.

PLOMER, WILLIAM, ed. *Kilverts diary: selection from the diary of the Rev. Francis Kilvert.* 3 vols. New ed. Jonathan Cape, 1960. Chatty diary of the 19th c.

STREET, A.G. *Farmer's glory.* Faber, 1932. Portrait of early 20th c. farming life in South Wiltshire by a writer whose many other books are also worth reading.

For Salisbury, see:

CHANDLER, JOHN. *Endless street: a history of Salisbury and its people.* Salisbury: Hobnob Press, 1983. Includes good bibliography, and two lists of names, c.1400.

ROYAL COMMISSION ON HISTORICAL MONUMENTS. *Ancient and historical monuments in the City of Salisbury, 1.* H.M.S.O., 1980. Includes notes on monumental heraldry.

There are many works on the Wiltshire textile industry. The following are amongst the most important:

MANN, J. DE. L. *The cloth industry in the West of England from 1640 to 1880.* Oxford U.P., 1971.

PONTING, KENNETH G. *The woollen industry of South-West England.* Bath: Adams & Dart, 1971.

RAMSAY, G.D. *The Wiltshire woollen industry in the sixteenth and seventeenth centuries.* 2nd ed. Frank Coss & Co., 1965.

ROGERS, K.H. 'Trowbridge clothiers and their houses, 1660-1800', in HARTE, NEGLEB BOYD, & PONTING, KENNETH G., eds. *Textile history and economic history: essays in honour of Miss Julia De Lacy Mann.* Manchester: Manchester University Press, 1973, 138-62.

PONTING, K.G. *Wool and water: Bradford-on-Avon and the River Frome.* Moonraker Press, 1975.

Wiltshire's industrial archaeology in general is treated in two works:

CORFIELD, M.C., ed. *A guide to the industrial archaeology of Wiltshire.* Trowbridge: Wiltshire County Council Library and Museum Service, for W.A.N.H.S., 1978.

SAWTELL, JOHN C., ed. *Wiltshire industrial archaeology.* Trowbridge: Wiltshire Industrial Archaeology Society, c.1970.

A number of local authors have written descriptive accounts of life in their times—for example, Richard Jefferies, Alfred Williams, Ida Gandy, A.G. Street and Ralph Whitlock. These are not genealogical works, and cannot be listed here; nevertheless, reading them will help to give you the 'flavour' of the county. The selection of histories listed above is merely intended to whet the appetite; many others could be suggested. Some are mentioned below; if you need further guidance, consult the works listed in section 2A.

2. BIBLIOGRAPHY AND ARCHIVES

A. BOOKS

The present work is primarily concerned with genealogy, and consequently omits many works of more general historical interest. To identify these, consult:

GODDARD, EDWARD H. *Wiltshire bibliography: a catalogue of printed books, pamphlets and articles bearing on the history, topography, and natural history of the county.* [Trowbridge]: Wilts Education Committee, 1929. This is continued by:

GREEN, ROSEMARY A.M. *A bibliography of printed works relating to Wiltshire, 1920-1960.* Trowbridge: Wiltshire County Council Library and Museum Service, 1975.

An abortive attempt to produce annual bibliographies was made in the late 1970s: *Wiltshire bibliography, 1976.* Trowbridge: Wiltshire Library and Museum Service, 1979.

There are now plans to produce a bibliography for 1960-90, and to issue annual bibliographies thereafter.

In addition, reviews of many books and articles (including newspaper articles) are to be found in *W.A.M.*, passim.

A major collection of Wiltshire books is held by the Wiltshire Archaeological and Natural History Society. Its catalogue has been published:

BELL, W. HEWARD, & GODDARD, E.H. *Catalogue of the printed books, pamphlets, mss. and maps in the library of the Wiltshire Archaeological and Natural History Society's museum at Devizes.* Devizes: Hurry and Pearson, 1894. 3 supplements published 1895-99. Additions to the library, both books and manuscripts, are regularly listed in *W.A.M.* For a brief description of the library, see:

'Wiltshire Archaeological and Natural History Society library', *W.F.H.S.* **28**, 1988, 25-6. See also *Wiltshire Local History Forum* **18**, 1991, 3-4.

A number of bibliographies, etc., for particular towns are available:

Calne
Calne: a select bibliography. [Calne?]: Wiltshire County Library, 1955.

Chippenham
WILTSHIRE LIBRARY AND MUSEUM SERVICE. *Chippenham: a bibliography.* Trowbridge: the Service, 1980.

Melksham
COOPER, G.S.B., THOMAS, C.A., & THOMAS, S.R. *The Melksham area: a guide to sources of historical information: an index to the Wiltshire Archaeological and Natural History Magazine, vols. 1-60 (1965).* Trowbridge: Wiltshire County Library, 1966.

COOPER, G.S.B., THOMAS, C.A., & THOMAS, S.R. *The Melksham area: a guide to sources of its history, pt.2: an index to the Trowbridge and N.Wilts Advertizer, 1854-79.* Trowbridge: Wiltshire County Library for Melksham and District Historical Association, 1970.

Swindon
COLE, JEAN A. 'Books about Swindon, old and new', *W.F.H.S.* **10**, 1983, 17-20.

TRAYHURN, R.J. 'Resources of the Swindon local history library', *Journal of the Bristol & Avon Family History Society*, **17**, 1979, 17-18.

Trowbridge
ISAAC, CHRISTINE. *Trowbridge: a bibliography.* Ealing: Ealing College of Higher Education, 1988.

B. ARCHIVES

Archival resources should not be examined until you have consulted all the printed material available. This will save you considerable time, and will also reduce the wear and tear on manuscripts—which are unique and irreplaceable. When you are ready to tackle the archives, the best place to begin is:

CARTER, BARBARA J. *Location of documents for Wiltshire parishes.* 7 vols. Swindon: the author, 1981. Supplemented by 'Location of documents for Wiltshire parishes: additions and alterations', *W.F.H.S.* **12**, 1983, 24-8. This is the essential guide to the location of original parish registers, churchwardens' accounts, manorial rolls, parochial rate lists, etc., etc.

The major archive repository for Wiltshire is the Wiltshire Record Office. Its holdings are briefly described in two works:

WILTSHIRE RECORD OFFICE. *Wiltshire records 1947-1987: a report on the work of the Wiltshire County Record Office.* [Trowbridge]: Wiltshire County Council, c.1987. Includes one-page listing of the major deposits.

COLE, JEAN A. 'The Wiltshire Record Office', *Family tree magazine*, **2**(5), 1986, 12.

Bibliography and Archives continued

The major guides to the Record Office include:

STEWART, PAMELA. *Guide to County Council, parish, poor law and other official records in the Wiltshire Record Office.* Wiltshire County Council guide to the Record Office, **2**. Trowbridge: Wiltshire County Council, 1961.

RATHBONE, MAURICE G. *Guide to the records in the custody of the Clerk of the Peace for Wiltshire.* Wiltshire County Council guide to the Record Office, **1**. 1959.

See also:

'The records of Quarter Sessions in the county of Wilts', in HISTORICAL MANUSCRIPTS COMMISSION *Report on manuscripts in various collections* **1**. Cd.784. H.M.S.O., 1901, 65-176.

'The county of Wilts', in HISTORICAL MANUSCRIPTS COMMISSION *Sixteenth report ...* Cd.2209. H.M.S.O., 1904, 95-6. Brief note on quarter session records. For other works on Quarter Sessions records, see below, section 15.

WILTSHIRE RECORD OFFICE. *Summary guide to private records in the Wiltshire County Record Office, County Hall, Trowbridge.* Trowbridge: Wiltshire County Council, 1969.

New accessions are regularly listed in:

'List of accessions to the County Record Office, County Hall, Trowbridge', *W.A.M.* **52**(187), 1947-.

A number of brief guides have been prepared for the use of researchers:

WILTSHIRE RECORD OFFICE. *Sources for the history of a Wiltshire family.* Rev. ed. Trowbridge: Wiltshire Library & Museum Service, 1983.

WILTSHIRE RECORD OFFICE. *Sources for the history of a Wiltshire parish.* Trowbridge: Wiltshire Library & Museum Service, 1980.

WILTSHIRE RECORD OFFICE. *Sources for the history of a Wiltshire building.* Trowbridge: Wiltshire Library & Museum Service, [198-].

For the diocesan record office formerly at Salisbury, now part of the County Record Office at Trowbridge, see:

STEWART, PAMELA. 'Salisbury Diocesan Record Office', *W.A.M.* **58**(210), 1962, 181-4.

EVERETT, C.R. 'The Sarum Diocesan records', *Salisbury Diocesan gazette* **52**, 1939, 213-8. Describes records of the Consistory Court.

STEWART, PAMELA. 'The Cathedral archives, Salisbury', *W.A.M.* **63**, 1968, 94-7.

Detailed guides to the diocesan archives are listed in section 13 below.

The archives of the Roman Catholic Diocese of Clifton, which includes Wiltshire, Gloucestershire and Somerset, are described in:

CLOSE, JUDITH. 'The archives of the Diocese of Clifton', *South Western Catholic history* **1**, 1983, 3-9.

BRADLEY, ANNE. 'Interim report on Clifton Diocesan archives deposited at Bristol Records Office', *South Western Catholic history* **4**, 1986, 6-11. Includes list of registers.

The antiquary Sir Thomas Phillipps collected many Wiltshire documents. See:

'Manuscript collections for Wiltshire in the possession of Sir Thomas Phillipps, Bart. ...', *W.A.M.* **1**(2), 1854, 97-104.

KITE, EDWARD. 'Wiltshire topography (1659-1843) with some notes on the late Sir Thomas Phillipps and his historical collections for the county', *W.N.Q.* **6**, 1908-10, 145-61. Includes pedigree of Phillipps, 16-19th c., lists material printed by Phillipps, and his manuscript collections.

3. JOURNALS AND NEWSPAPERS

Every genealogist with ancestors from Wiltshire should join the Wiltshire Family History Society. It will enable you to make contact with others who may be researching the same lines. The Society's journal is simply entitled:

Wiltshire Family History Society. Swindon: the Society, 1981-.

This regularly lists new members, together with the names of families they are researching. For a more comprehensive listing of names currently being researched, see:

MILLER, BARRY. *Wiltshire families directory.* Easterton: W.F.H.S., 1991.

For a somewhat dated description of the Society's activities, see:

'Wiltshire Family History Society', *Family tree magazine* 1(4), 1985, 16 and 1(5), 1985, 26.

The major historical journal for Wiltshire, which includes many works of genealogical interest, is:

Wiltshire Archaeological and Natural History magazine. 71 vols. 1853-1976. From vol.70/71, 1975-6, became *The Wiltshire Archaeological magazine.* From vol.76, 1981, reverted to original title.

This is indexed in:

JACKSON, J.E. 'General index to the Wiltshire Archaeological and Natural History Magazine, from its commencement in A.D. 1853', *W.A.M.* 8(24), 1864, i-lvii.

'General index to the Wiltshire Archaeological and Natural History Magazine, vols.IX to XVI', *W.A.M.* 16, 1876, i-lxxii.

'General index to the Wiltshire Archaeological and Natural History Magazine, vols.XVII to XXIV', *W.A.M.* 24, 1889, i-lxvi.

'Wiltshire Archaeological and Natural History Magazine: general index to ... volume XXV to XXXII, 1890-1902', *W.A.M.* 32, 382-551.

Of even greater value to the genealogist is:

Wiltshire notes and queries: an illustrated quarterly antiquarian and genealogical magazine. 8 vols. Devizes: George Simpson, jun.; London: Elliot Stock, 1896-1916.

The publications of record societies frequently include works vital to the genealogist; many are listed in this bibliography. The major series for Wiltshire is:

Wiltshire Archaeological and Natural History Society. Records Branch. Devizes: the Society, 1939-. Became *Wiltshire Record Society* from vol.23-, 1969-.

The work of the Wiltshire Record Society is briefly discussed in:

CHANDLER, JOHN. 'Wiltshire Record Society 50th anniversary', *W.F.H.S.* 33, 1989, 20-21.

Notes and news on current activities in Wiltshire local history are contained in *Wiltshire Local History Forum newsletter* 1985-.

A useful journal covering the Salisbury area is:

The Hatcher review. Salisbury: Hatcher Society, 1976-.

Wiltshire extracts from a major topographical journal of the 18th century are presented in:

'Extracts from the *Gentlemans magazine* relating to Wiltshire', *W.N.Q.* 1, 1893-5, 211-19, 265-70, 298-304, 363-7, 397-404, 442-8, 490-98 & 543-9; 2, 1896-8, 18-24, 53-60, 116-25 & 222-8; 8, 1914-16, 225-8, 261-6, 346-50, 401-4, 439-43 & 502-6. 18th c., not continued.

For Wiltshire newspapers, see the lists in:

WELLS, ROSEMARY. *Newsplan: report of the pilot project in the South West.* Library and Information Research Report 38, British Library, 1986.

WILTSHIRE LIBRARY AND MUSEUM SERVICE. *Newspapers held on microfilm.* 1992.

BLUHM, R.K., ed. *Bibliography of British newspapers: Wiltshire.* Library Association. Reference, Special & Information Section, 1975.

4. BIOGRAPHICAL DICTIONARIES

Biographical dictionaries provide brief biographical information on the individuals listed. Many such dictionaries are available, and are invaluable to the genealogist. For general guidance on identifying them, consult *English genealogy: an introductory bibliography*. Those for Wiltshire, listed chronologically, include:

STRATFORD, JOSEPH. *Wiltshire and its worthies: notes topographical and biographical*. Salisbury: Brown, 1882.

Wiltshire and some neighbouring records: historical, biographical and pictorial. Allan North, [190-?].

DORLING, E.E. *Wilts and Dorset at the opening of the 20th century: contemporary biographies*. Brighton: W.T. Pike & Co., 1906. Reprinted as *A dictionary of Edwardian biography: Wiltshire*. Edinburgh: Peter Bell, 1983.

GASKILL, W. *Wiltshire leaders, social and political*. Queenhithe Printing, [1906]. 63 biographies.

STACEY, C. *Men of the West: a pictorial who's who of the distinguished, eminent and famous men of the West Country, embracing the counties of Cornwall, Devon, Somerset, Dorset, Wilts and Gloucester, including the city of Bristol*. Claude Stacey Ltd., 1926.

Who's who in Wiltshire. Hereford: Wilson & Philips, 1934.

GREENWOOD, DOUGLAS. *Wessex has their bones: who's buried where in Dorset, Hampshire, the Isle of Wight and Wiltshire*. Wimborne: Roy Gasson Associates, 1985. Brief biographies.

In addition, *W.A.M.* regularly publishes a series of 'Wiltshire obituaries', which should be consulted for the lives of leading Wiltshiremen of the 19th and 20th centuries.

Many Wiltshire portraits are listed in:

A catalogue of some portraits and other prints having to do with the county of Wilts, from the collection of Ambrose Tucker. Salisbury: Bennett Bros., 1908.

Two lists of the Wiltshire nobility and gentry may also be worth consulting:

'Nobles and gentry in Wiltshire in the time of Henry VII', *Topographer* 2, 1790, 96-107. Notes on many families, with a list of Justices of the Peace, 1576.

'The nobility and gentry of Wiltshire, 1673', *W.N.Q.* 6, 1908-10, 25-31. See also 88. List.

5. OCCUPATIONAL SOURCES, ETC.

There are many works offering biographical information on persons of particular occupations. These are listed here. The term 'occupation' has been interpreted broadly, to include status groups such as bankrupts, freemasons, etc. For clergymen, see section 13, members of parliament and local government officers, section 15, teachers and students, section 16.

Apothecaries

WHITTET, T.D. 'Wiltshire apothecaries tokens and their issuers', *W.A.M.* **81**, 1987, 74-9. Includes biographical notes.

Apprentices

CARTER, B.J. 'Apprentices of the Broad Town charity', *W.F.H.S.* **28**, 1988, 28-32; **29**, 1988, 18-20; **30**, 1988, 20-22; **31**, 1988, 20-22; **33**, 1989, 28-30. Lists the surnames of those apprenticed by this charity, which had a Wiltshire-wide remit, 1714-1909.

DALE, CHRISTABEL, ed. *Wiltshire apprentices and their masters, 1710-1760*. W.R.S., **17**, 1961. Important; from the apprenticeship registers of the Inland Revenue.

HUNT, JULIA. 'Oxford city apprentices, 1697-1800', *W.F.H.S.* **35**, 1989, 22-3. From Wiltshire.

Authors

GODDARD, E.H. 'Existing material for Wiltshire bibliography', *W.A.M.* **40**(129), 1918, 209-32 and 272. Primarily a list of Wiltshire authors.

Bankrupts

CARTER, BARBARA. 'Wiltshire bankrupts', *W.F.H.S.* **34**, 1989, 16-17. List, 1731-55, from the *Gentlemans magazine*.

Bell Founders

L., H. 'Salisbury bell foundry', *W.N.Q.* **1**, 1893-5, 44. See also 92 & 136. Includes list of bell founders, 15-18th c.

Carriers

GREENING, ALAN. 'Nineteenth century carriers in North Wiltshire', *W.A.M.* **66**, 1971, 162-76. Includes lists.

Clockmakers

CUNNINGTON, B.H. 'Clock and watch makers of Wiltshire of the 17th and 18th centuries', *W.A.M.* **48**(169), 1938, 313-7. See also **50**(177), 1942, 92-4. List.

Occupational Sources continued

Clockmakers *continued*

KITE, EDWARD. 'Some old Wiltshire clocks and clockmakers', *W.N.Q.* **6**, 1908-10, 309-21. Listed by place, with genealogical notes.

SNELL, MICHAEL. *Clocks and clockmakers of Salisbury: 600 years of skill and invention.* Salisbury: Hobnob Press, 1986. Lists clockmakers of Salisbury and South Wiltshire, giving much biographical information.

Criminals

COLE, JEAN. 'Was your ancestor a criminal?', *W.F.H.S.* **35**, 1989, 8-9. Lists Wiltshire prisoners on a prison hulk at Sheerness, Kent, 1823, and at Fisherton gaol, 1842.

WAYLEN, J. *The highwaymen of Wiltshire or, a narrative of the adventurous career and untimely end of divers freebooters and smugglers in this and the adjoining counties.* Devizes: N.B. Randle, 1845. Reprinted E. & W. Books, 1970.

Fisherton gaol: statistics of crime from 1801 to 1850. Salisbury: Frederick A. Blake, 1855. Includes notes on many trials.

Drapers

'Draper Guild, Devizes: admissions of freemen (1614-1730)', *W.N.Q.* **8**, 1914-16, 551-2.

Freemasons

ASHLEY, R.J. *Freemasonry in Marlborough: a history of the Methuen Chapter, from 1883 to 1983.* [Marlborough: The Chapter], 1983. Gives many names.

AYLING, KENNETH G. *Moose in Wessex.* Bristol: Regional Grand Lodge of Wessex, 1963. History of the Loyal Order of Moose, 1926-63, primarily in Dorset, Wiltshire and Hampshire, giving many names—although unfortunately no index.

GOLDNEY, FREDERICK HASTINGS. *A history of freemasonry in Wiltshire ...* Virtue & Co., 1880. Includes many lists of names.

TUCKETT, J.E.S. *Notes of freemasonry in the town of Marlborough, 1768-1834.* Marlborough: Lucy & Co., 1910. Gives many names.

Wiltshire Lodge of Fidelity no.663: ancient free and accepted masons, Devizes: centenary celebration, ... 1956. [Devizes]: the Lodge, 1956. Gives many names of members, etc.

Innkeepers

CUNDICK, REG. *The inns and taverns of Warminster.* Warminster: Warminster History Society, 1987. Gives names of some innkeepers.

Insurance Policy Holders

REDSTONE, ALAN. 'Insurance policy holders', *Journal of the Bristol & Avon Family History Society* **8**, 1977, 15-26. In Wiltshire. Alphabetical list.

Wiltshire insurance policy holders. [Bristol]: Bristol & Avon Family History Society, [1979?]. Lists Sun Fire Office policy holders, 18th c.

See also Mill Owners.

Medical Men

HASKINS, CHARLES. *The history of Salisbury Infirmary, founded by Anthony Lord Feversham, A.D.1766.* Salisbury & District Infirmary & Hospital League, 1922. Includes list of officers since 1767.

Mill Owners

PONTING, K.G. 'Wiltshire woollen mills: insurance returns, 1753-1771', *W.A.M.* **69**, 1974, 161-72. Lists mill owners.

Millers

ROGERS, K.H. *Wiltshire and Somerset woollen mills.* Edington: Pasold Research Fund, 1976. Includes gazetteer, giving names of many millers.

Mollusc Collectors

HEGINBOTHOM, C.D. 'Wiltshire mollusc collectors', *W.A.M.* **51**(185), 1946, 457-63. Brief biographical sketches, 18-20th c.

Patentees

PROSSER, RICHARD B. 'A list of Wiltshire patentees', *W.N.Q.* **1**, 1893-5, 3-6, 65-9 & 97-101. 17-19th c.

Photographers

HOWELL, DANNY. 'Some of Warminster's early photographers', *Wiltshire Local History Forum newsletter* **19**, 1991, 4-5. Brief biographical notes.

Pipemakers

ATKINSON, D.R. 'Clay tobacco pipes and pipemakers of Marlborough', *W.A.M.* **60**, 1965, 85-95. Includes list with brief biographical notes.

ATKINSON, D.R. 'Clay tobacco pipes and pipemakers of Salisbury, Wiltshire', *W.A.M.* **65**, 1970, 177-89. Includes some names.

ATKINSON, D.R. 'Further notes on clay tobacco pipes and pipemakers from the Marlborough and Salisbury districts', *W.A.M.* **67**, 1972, 149-56. Includes biographical notes.

Occupational Sources continued

Pipemakers continued

ATKINSON, D. 'More Wiltshire clay tobacco pipe varieties', *W.A.M.* **72/3**, 1980, 67-74. Includes some names.

Police

COLLINS, BRIAN. 'Wiltshire constabulary', *W.F.H.S.* **19**, 1985, 58-9. Lists police archives of the 19th c.

Quarrymen

TUCKER, ROGER J. *Some notable Wiltshire quarrymen.* Bristol: Free Troglophile Association, [197-?]. Includes pedigree, 19-20th c., showing relationship of Dancey, Pinnock, Barnett, and Light.

Soldiers and Militiamen, etc.

Many Wiltshiremen served in either the army, or the militia, and much information on them is available in the various regimental histories, honour rolls, etc., which have been published. These cannot all be listed here. The works included below include only those publications which provide lists of officers and men, and are therefore likely to be of genealogical value. The list is in rough chronological order.

TITFORD, JOHN S. 'Militia records/coroners accounts', *W.F.H.S.* **20**, 1986, 4. Brief note on Wiltshire sources for militia men.

KENRICK, N.C.E. *The story of the Wiltshire Regiment (Duke of Edinburgh's): the 62nd and 99th Foot (1756-1959), the Militia and the Territorials, the service battalions and all others who have served or been affiliated with the Moonrakers.* Aldershot: Gale and Polden, 1963. Includes biographical notes on colonels, etc.

LAWES, EDWARD. 'Searching the Wiltshire regiments of militia, 1780-1814', *W.F.H.S.* **5**, 1982, 10-15. General discussion of militia records; includes names of volunteers from Woodford and Durnsford, 1803.

GRAHAM, HENRY. *The annals of the Yeomanry Cavalry of Wiltshire ...* 2 vols. Devizes: Geo. Simpson, 1908. Includes lists of officers and men. v.1. 1794-1884. v.2. 1884-93. v.2(2). 1893-1908.

WILLIAMS, J. ROBERT. 'Wiltshire veterans of the 66th Foot', *W.F.H.S.* **13**, 1984, 18-24 & **15**, 1984, 5-9. List, 1800-1840.

WILLIAMS, J. ROBERT. 'Wiltshire veterans of the 41st Foot', *W.F.H.S.* **10**, 1983, 24-9. Lists Chelsea out-pensioners in Wiltshire, 1806-38.

Soldiers and Militiamen, etc. continued

RAVENHILL, W.W. 'The Wiltshire Regiment for Wiltshire', *W.A.M.* **17**, 1878, 192-234 & 364-6. Includes list of officers from the *Army list*, 1814.

GIBNEY, R.T. *The history of the 1st Batt. Wilts Volunteers, from 1861 to 1885.* W.H. Allen & Co., 1888. Includes extracts from *Army lists* giving many names.

HARFIELD, A.G. 'The great volunteer review at Salisbury on 29th May 1867', *Journal of the Society for Army Historical Research* **45**, 1967, 149-68. Includes names of many officers.

A pictorial souvenir of the Duke of Edinburgh's 2nd Battalion 4th Wiltshire Regiment and history of the 62nd and 99th Foot, now the 1st and 2nd Battalions. Poona, India, 1915. Bombay: British Historical and Art Publishing Co., 1915. Includes nominal roll, with many portraits.

PLATT, J.R.I. *The Royal Wiltshire Yeomanry (Prince of Wales's Own) 1907-1967.* Garnstone Press, 1972. Includes an alphabetical list of officers, 1908-67.

Soldiers died in the Great War, 1914-19. Pt.58. The Duke of Edinburgh's (Wiltshire Regiment). H.M.S.O., 1921. Reprinted Polstead: J.B. Hayward & Son, 1989.

SHEPHERD, W.S. *The 2nd Battalion Wiltshire Regiment (99th): a record of their fighting in the Great War, 1914-18.* Aldershot: Gale & Polden, 1927. Includes list of 80 officers killed, and 110 honours won by officers and men.

KNUBLEY, E.P. *The record of the parish of Steeple Ashton, including the tithing of Great Hinton, in the county of Wilts, in relation to the Great War, 1914-1919.* Trowbridge: Massey & Co., 1919. Includes roll of honour, with notes on service.

BAVIN, W.D. *Swindon's war record.* [ ], 1922. Includes roll of honour and list of men who served.

SANDERS, HARRY. *Trowbridge roll of honour, 1914-1918.* Trowbridge: B. Lansdown and Sons, [1919?].

PITT, P.W. *Royal Wilts: the history of the Royal Wiltshire Yeomanry, 1920-1945.* Burrup, Mathieson & Co., 1946. Includes list of personnel.

PARSONS, A.D., ROBBINS, D.I.M., AND GILSON, D.C. *The maroon square: a history of the 4th Battalion, the Wiltshire Regiment (Duke of Edinburgh's) in North-West Europe, 1939-1946.* Franey & Co., [1955]. Includes extensive list of battle casualties.

Occupational Sources *continued*

Soldiers and Militiamen, etc. *continued*

MACKAY, E.A., ed. *The history of the Wiltshire Home Guard*. [Trowbridge]: Wiltshire Regiment Old Comrades Association, 1946. Includes many names.

MCMATH, J.S. *The Fifth Battalion the Wiltshire Regiment in North-West Europe, June 1944 to May 1945*. Whitefriars Press, [194-?]. Includes roll of honour.

Swan Owners

MAYO, C.H. 'Swans on the Salisbury Avon, and the Dorset Stour', *Notes & queries for Somerset & Dorset* 13, 1913, 297-313. Includes list of 135 owners.

Tailors

HASKINS, C. 'The original bederoll of the Salisbury tailor's guild', *W.A.M.* 39(125), 1916, 375-9. Lists 15th c. names.

Tradesmen

WILLIAMS, N.J., ed. *Tradesmen in early Stuart Wiltshire: a miscellany*. W.R.S. 15, 1960. Contents: Fines made before the Clerk of the Market of the King's Household in Wiltshire, 1607; Lenten recognizances taken in Wiltshire, 1620; Informations relating to Wiltshire lodged in the Court of Exchequer in the reign of James I; Licensed retailers of tobacco, 1637.

In an age when coins were in short supply, a variety of tradesmen issued their own tokens.

Tradesmen *continued*

There are a number of studies of these tokens for Wiltshire, providing information which may be of genealogical value:

AKERMAN, JOHN YONGE. *A list of tokens issued by Wiltshire tradesmen in the seventeenth century*. Hazlitt tracts, 2(3), 1846. Reprinted from the *Numismatic chronicle* 8, 1845, 97-115.

BOYNE, WILLIAM. 'Wiltshire tradesmen's tokens', *W.A.M.* 6(16), 1860, 75-91. Listed by place of issue.

KEMPSON, E.G.H. *Wiltshire XVII century tokens.* Salisbury: C.M. Rowe, 1978.

WILLIS, F.M. *Catalogue of the collection of Wiltshire trade tokens in the Museum of the Wiltshire Archaeological and Natural History Society at Devizes*. Devizes: W.A.N.H.S., 1893. Reprinted from *W.A.M.* 26(78), 1892, 391-404. See also 30(92), 1899, 304-6. 17th c.

ROWE, C.M. *Salisbury's local coinage (seventeenth century trade tokens)*. Salisbury: Tisbury Printing Works, 1966.

ROWE, C.M. 'Salisbury's token currency', *Hatcher review* 1(4), 1977, 12-24. Names of many traders, especially innkeepers.

Weavers

RADCLIFFE, F.R.Y. 'List of Wiltshiremen extracted from the minute books of the Company of Weavers of London, 1653-1674', *W.A.M.* 38(122), 1914, 572-5.

6. HERALDIC VISITATIONS, etc.

In the sixteenth and seventeenth centuries, the heralds undertook 'visitations' of the counties in order to determine the right of gentry to bear heraldic arms. This involved the compilation of pedigrees for most gentle families. The heralds' returns continue to be important sources of genealogical information; for Wiltshire, see:

CARRINGTON, F.A. 'The heralds' visitations of Wiltshire and the pedigrees of Wiltshire families', *W.A.M.* 2(6), 1855, 356-86. Lists of pedigrees, etc., from all visitations, with detailed discussion.

TALBOT, C.H. 'Benolt's visitation of Wilts', *W.N.Q.* 2, 1896-8, 303-13. See also 368-70. Brief pedigrees.

METCALFE, WALTER C., ed. *The visitation of Wiltshire, 1565, by William Harvey, Clarenceux King of Arms, (Harleian ms. 1565), together with additional Wiltshire pedigrees (from various Harleian mss.).* Exeter: William Pollard & Co., 1897.

SQUIBB, G.D., ed. *Wiltshire visitation pedigrees, 1623, with additional pedigrees and arms collected by Thomas Lyte of Lyte's Cary, Co.Somerset, 1628.* Harleian Society Publications, 1954, 105-6.

MARSHALL, GEORGE W., ed. *The visitation of Wiltshire, 1623.* George Bell & Sons, 1882. This supersedes: [PHILLIPPS, THOMAS], ed. *Visitatio heraldica comitatus Wiltoniae, A.D. 1623.* [Middle Hill]: Typis Medio-Montanis, 1828.

HOPPER, CLARENCE. 'Wiltshire arms and descents', *W.A.M.* 9(27), 1866, 223-31. 17th c. list of Wiltshire families in the 1620 visitations of other counties.

For a later collection of heraldic arms, see:
SCHOMBERG, A. 'Wiltshire arms in 1716', *W.A.M.* 3, 1899-1901, 471-3. See also 4, 1902-4, 49-53. Extracts of Wiltshire interest from the *Grammar of heraldry*, 1716.

A modern collection of manuscript pedigrees, mostly relating to North Wiltshire families, is listed in:
CARTER, N.M.G. 'Pedigrees in Cricklade Museum', *W.A.M.* 61, 1966, 100-101. See also 66, 1971, 185-6.

7. FAMILY HISTORIES

A considerable amount of research on Wiltshire family history has been published. This list includes published books and journal articles; it does not, however, include the innumerable notes and queries published in journals such as *W.F.H.S.*, except where substantial information is provided. Studies which remain unpublished are not listed.

Amiel
See Merryweather

Annett
ANNETTE, F.H. 'Annetts and Annett in the Wessex region', *W.F.H.S.* 6, 1982, 4-6. In Wiltshire, Berkshire, Hampshire and Gloucestershire. 18th c.

Arundell
ARUNDELL, LORD. *Notes ... on the family history.* ed. Edward Doran Webb. Longmans Green & Co., 1916. Arundell of Wardour, 16-20th c.

WALSH, V. HUSSEY. 'The Arundells of Wardour', in DRYDEN, ALICE, ed. *Memorials of old Wiltshire.* Bemrose and Sons, 1906, 95-106. 16-19th c.

w., B.D. *Wardour and the Arundells not so long ago.* [ ]: [ ], 1982. 19-20th c.

YEATMAN, JOHN PYM. *The early genealogical history of the house of Arundell, being an account of the origin of the families of Montgomery, Albini, Fitzalan, and Howard, from the time of the conquest of Normandy by Rollo the Great.* Mitchell & Hughes, 1882.

Ayer
See Eyre

Ayliffe
JACKSON, J.E. 'The Ayliffes of Grittenham', *W.A.M.* 21(62), 1884, 194-210. 17-18th c.

Baker
See De Boteville

Barnes
See Tugwell

Barrett
BARRETT, DAN E. *Barrett: our family name.* Ontario: the author, c.1981.

Batt
'The English ancestry of the families of Batt and Byley, of Salisbury, Massachusetts', *W.N.Q.* 2, 1896-8, 577-83; 3, 1899-1901, 35-40. Includes pedigree of Batt, 16-17th c., with wills, etc.

Batt *continued*

LEA, J. HENRY. *The English ancestry of the families of Batt and Biley*. Boston: David Clapp, 1897. Reprinted from *New England Historical and Genealogical Register*. Includes 17th c. pedigree, with wills and parish register extracts.

Baugh
See De Boteville

Bayntun
BAYNTUN-COWARD, HYLTON, ed. *Notes on the Bayntun family*. Bath: George Bayntun, 1977. Includes pedigrees, medieval-20th c.

Beach
See Sadler

Beckford
GREGORY, W. *The Beckford family: reminiscences of Fonthill Abbey and Lansdown Tower*. Bath: Queen Square Library, 1887. 18-19th c.
MELVILLE, LEWIS. *The life and letters of William Beckford of Fonthill*. William Heinemans, 1910. Includes notes on family, 16-18th c.

Berrett
BERRETT, LA MAR C. *Down Berrett Lane*. 2 vols. Orem, Utah: John Watts Family Organization, 1980. Steeple Ashton and U.S.A., 17-20th c.

Besils
DUNLOP, J. RENTON. 'Pedigree of the Besils family of Gloucestershire, Wiltshire, Devonshire, Berkshire and Somerset', *M.G.H.* 5th series **5**, 1923-5, 63-82. Medieval.

Bettesthorne
COLLINS, S.M. 'A Wiltshire ancestor for Her Majesty the Queen', *W.A.M.* **50**(180), 1943, 375-8. Medieval pedigree of Bettesthorne.

Biley
See Batt

Billet
CLARKE, PHILIP J. 'The Billets of North Wraxall', *W.F.H.S.* **27**, 1987, 26-8. See also **39**, 1990, 22-3. Emigrants to Canada. Includes pedigree, 18-19th c.

Blake
BLAKE, MARK. 'Some early Wiltshire emigrants to Australia', *Hatcher review* **2**(17), 1984, 328-34. Blake family; 19th c.

Blount
'Blount of Gynge Joyberd Laundry, Essex, Penkridge, Staffs., Kingston Blount, Oxon., Putteridge, Herts., and Beversbrook and Calston, Wilts.', *M.G.H.* 5th series **7**, 1929-31, 120-24. 12-15th c. pedigree.

Bonham
KIDSTON, GEORGE JARDINE. *The Bonhams of Wiltshire and Essex*. Devizes: C.H. Woodward, 1948. 14-18th c.
KIDSTON, GEORGE. 'The Bonham family', *Notes & Queries for Somerset & Dorset* **19**, 1929, 185-90. Wiltshire family.

Botfield
See De Boteville

Boucher
BOUCHER, R. 'Boucher', *W.N.Q.* **5**, 1902-5, 142-4. 18th c., includes wills and parish register extracts.
See also Cromwell

Bourne
See Eyre

Bouveries
PLEYDELL-BOUVERIE, JACOB. 'Laurens Des Bouveries (1536-1610), his descendents, and the Huguenot connection', *Hatcher review* **2**(19), 1985, 411-20. Includes pedigree, 16-18th c.

Bower
BOWER, H.B. *Bower of Claremont, Donhead, Dorchester, Lostwithiel and Weymouth*. Fleet: E. Dwelly, 1929. Donhead, Wiltshire; Claremont, Devon; Dorchester and Weymouth, Dorset, and Lostwithiel, Cornwall.

Brethers
See Goldesborough

Bridgeman
LOVELOCK, SVE. 'Bridgeman trail', *W.F.H.S.* **31**, 1988, 34-6. Includes pedigree, 17-19th c.

Brotherhood
LELEUX, SYDNEY A. *Brotherhoods, engineers*. Dawlish: David & Charles, 1965. Includes pedigree of Brotherhood family, 19-20th c.

Brown
COWARD, EDWARD. 'Notes on farming families of the 19th century in Wiltshire', *W.A.M.* **45**(154), 1931, 336-41. Notes on Brown, Stratton and a number of other families.

Family Histories continued

Browne
MORTON, EDWARD. *The Browne family of Kington St.Michael, Co.Wilts* ... ed. Charles W. Marshall. Exeter: the author, 1983. 16-20th c.

Buckeridge
DYER, ANTHONY STEPHEN. 'Buckeridge family', *W.N.Q.* **6**, 1908-10, 571-2. 17-18th c.

Buckland
NORGATE, MARTIN. 'Buckland et al., pipemakers in Melksham', *W.A.M.* **78**, 1983, 125-7. Buckland family, 17-18th c.

Burton
NAISH, SANDRA. 'Burton family of Tisbury', *W.F.H.S.* **28**, 1988, 12-15. Includes pedigree, 18-20th c.

Bush
'Paul Bush, the last rector of Edington and first bishop of Bristol', *W.N.Q.* **4**, 1902-4, 97-107 & 145-56. See also 426-7. Includes pedigree, 16th c., monumental inscription, and various Bush wills.

Byley
See Batt

Calston
Littlecote. Hatchard, 1900. Partly a history of the Calston, Darrell and Popham families.

Chandler
'The Chandlers of Wiltshire', *W.N.Q.* **1**, 1893-5, 352-4. See also 410-13 & 448. 17th c. emigrants to America.
See also Merryweather

Chapman
K., A. 'Chapman of Tetbury', *W.N.Q.* **1**, 1893-5, 372-3. 17th c.

Cheyne
FANSHAWE, H., & PRIDEAUX, F.B. 'Cheyne of Dorset and Wilts', *Notes & Queries* **153**, 1927, 463. See also 388, and **155**, 1928, 301, 336-7 & 371.

Child
LIGHT, M.E. 'Heddington and the Child family', *W.N.Q.* **2**, 1896-8, 207-18 & 261-71. See also 301-2. 15-18th c.

Chivers
JONES, WIN. 'The story of John Chivers and his wife Mary Ann, nee Gardiner, their ancestors, descendants, and the families they married into', *W.F.H.S.* **7**, 1982, 12-17. 19th c., Wiltshire and Australia.

Clutterbuck
'Clutterbuck of Hardenhuish', *W.N.Q.* **1**, 1893-5, 304-6. See also 517-8. 18-19th c.

Coleraine
MELLOR, A. SHAW. 'The Coleraine family of Longford', *W.A.M.* **52**(189), 1948, 328-37. 17-18th c.

Collier
BENSON, R. *Memoirs of the life and writings of the Rev. Arthur Collier, M.A., rector of Langford Magna in the County of Wilts from A.D. 1704 to A.D. 1732, with some account of his family.* Edward Lumley, 1837.

Combe
VON ROEMER, MARY. 'Notes on the descendants of Edward Combe of Bridsor in Tisbury', *W.N.Q.* **8**, 1914-16, 63-73 & 100-9. 16-18th c.
VON ROEMER, MARY. 'Notes on the lineage of Richard de Combe, lord of Fitelton, Combe and Todeworth, sheriff of Wilts, 18 Edward I', *W.N.Q.* **7**, 1911-13, 433-44 & 499-511. 13-16th c.

Combes
COMBES, LAWRENCE. 'The Wiltshire Combes family', *W.F.H.S.* **6**, 1982, 13-15. Medieval-20th c.

Corr
S., J. 'Corr of Aldbourne', *W.N.Q.* **4**, 1902-4, 410-14. 18th c.

Cottle
COTTELL, WILLIAM HENRY. *A history of the Cotel, Cottell, or Cottle family, of Devon, Somerset, Cornwall and Wilts, compiled from county histories, heralds visitations, etc.* Taylor & Co., 1871.
COTTELL, WILLIAM HENRY. *Pedigree of the family of Cotell, Cotele, Cottell, or Cottle, of the counties of Devon, Somerset, Cornwall and Wilts.* Mitchell & Hughes, [1891].

Courtenay
See Rogers

Crane
See Cromwell

Cresswell

CAMPBELL, GWLADYS. *The web of fortune: the narrative of an English family from the twelfth to the twentieth century.* Neville Spearman, 1965. Cresswell family.

Cromwell

BOUCHER, R. 'Oliver Cromwell's Wiltshire relations', *W.N.Q.* **7**, 1911-13, 25-32. Cromwell, Boucher and Crane families, 17th c.

SCHOMBERG, ARTHUR. 'Cromwell', *M.G.H.* 5th series **5**, 1923-5, 86-7. Extracts from Seend parish register, 17-18th c.

Cullimore

See Merryweather

Cunnington

CUNNINGTON, R.H. 'The Cunningtons of Wiltshire', *W.A.M.* **55**(200), 1954, 211-36. 18-19th c.

Danvers

MACNAMARA, F.N. *Memorials of the Danvers family (of Dauntsey and Culworth), their ancestors and descendants, from the Conquest till the termination of the eighteenth century ...* Hardy & Page, 1895. Dauntsey, Wiltshire; Culworth, Northamptonshire, Buckinghamshire and Oxfordshire, etc., includes pedigrees.

USHFORTH, G. MCN. 'The story of Dauntsey', *Bristol & Gloucestershire Archaeological Society transactions* **50**, 1928, 325-51. Danvers family; includes pedigree, 14-17th c.

LADE, J.J. 'The Yorkshire estate of the Danvers of Dauntsey', *W.A.M.* **50**(179), 1943, 214-8. 17th c.

Darrell

See Calston

D'Aubeney

ROUND, J. HORACE. 'A D'Aubeney cadet', *Ancestor* **12**, 1904, 149-51. 12-13th c.

Davys

FLETCHER, W.G. DIMOCK. 'Pedigree of Davys of Tisbury, Co.Wilts., of Rempstone, Co.Nottingham, and of Castle Donington and Loughborough, Co.Leicester', *Genealogist* **5**, 1881, 25-32. 16-19th c.

Dawson

See Massy-Dawson

De Boteville

BOTFIELD, BERIAH. *Stemmata Botevilliana: memorials of the families of De Boteville, Thynne and Botfield in the counties of Salop and Wilts.* J.B. Nichols and Sons, 1858. Also includes pedigrees of Leighton, Higgons, Haynes, Lake, Montgomery, Gresham, Baugh, Baker, Greve, and Hector families, with numerous extracts from original sources, medieval-19th c.

De Chyrebury

H[EATHCOTE], T.G.J. 'De Chyrebury of Seend', *W.N.Q.* **4**, 1902-4, 414-6. See also **5**, 1905-7, 43-6 & 86-8. Medieval.

De Dunstanville

BENSON, J. 'The De Dunstanvilles', *Devon & Cornwall notes & queries* **20**, 1938-9, 194-204. Of Devon, Shropshire, Sussex and Wiltshire; includes medieval pedigree.

Deverell

DEVERILL, PENELOPE. 'The medieval Deverells of Wilts and Bucks', *Origins: magazine of the Buckinghamshire Family History Society*, **15**(4) 1991, 95-6.

Dicke

See Dyer

Digges

See Harington

Drew

KITE, E. 'Drew of Southbroom', *W.N.Q.* **7**, 1911-13, 303-8 & 441-8. 16-17th c., includes extracts from Devizes parish registers, etc.

Dugdale

SCHOMBERG, A. 'Dugdale of Seend, Co.Wilts', *M.G.H.* 2nd series **2**, 1888, 128. Pedigree, 16-17th c.

SCHOMBERG, ARTHUR. 'Dugdale of Wilts', *W.N.Q.* **1**, 1893-5, 174-5 & 194-200. See also **3**, 1899-1901, 87-90, 127-9, 179-81 & 517-8; **4**, 1902-4, 315-20; **5**, 1905-7, 473 & 474. Reprinted as *Dugdale of Seend.* Devizes: George Simpson & Co., 1924. Includes pedigree, 16-18th c., wills, monumental inscriptions, parish register extracts, deeds, etc.

Duke

DUKE, R.E.H. 'An account of the family of Duke of Lake', *W.N.Q.* **8**, 1914-16, 193-205, 241-51 & 289-300. See also 426. 15-19th c., includes folded pedigrees.

Family Histories continued

Duket
DUCKETT, SIR G.F. *Duchetiana: or history and genealogical memoirs of the family of Duket from the Norman conquest to the present time, in the counties of Lincoln, Westmorland, Wilts, Cambridge, and Buckingham* ... 2nd ed. J. Russell Smith, 1874. Includes pedigrees and many original sources.

Dunford
MECHAM, LILLIE DUNFORD. *Dunford genealogy.* Logan, Utah: the author, [198-?]. Trowbridge and U.S.A., 18-20th c.

Dunsdon
GODDARD, J.R. *The Dunsdon family in Steeple Ashton, 1702-1885.* Newbury: [privately printed], c.1984. Includes pedigrees.

Dyer
'The origin of the Swinnerton Dyers, Baronets', *M.G.H.* 4th series 1, 1906, 316-21. See also 4th series 2, 1908, 45, 70 & 93-4. Somerset and Wiltshire; includes pedigree, 16-17th c., with wills of Rolfe, Dicke and Gerle.

Ellis
BAKER, THOS. H. 'Ellis of Wilts', *W.N.Q.* 3, 1899-1901, 45-6. See also 2, 1896-8, 436 & 484. Extracts from Mere parish register, 17th c.

Ellison
See Smith

Elton
See Mayo

Englefield
TRAPPES-LOMAX, T.B. 'The Englefields and their contribution to the survival of the faith in Berkshire, Wiltshire, Hampshire, and Leicestershire', *Biographical studies* 1, 1951, 131-48. Roman Catholic family.

Erasmus
See Rudman

Estcourt
LIGHT, MARY E. 'Estcourt of Swinley', *W.N.Q.* 2, 1896-8, 351-7 & 399-408. 17-18th c.
SYMONDS, W. 'Estcourt of Salisbury, Rollestone and Long Newnton', *W.N.Q.* 5, 1905-7, 325-8. 17th c.

Evans
MANLEY, F.H. 'The Evans family of North Wiltshire', *W.A.M.* 43(143), 1925, 168-74. 17-18th c.

Evelyn
EVELYN, HELEN. *The history of the Evelyn family.* Evelyn Nash, 1915. Surrey and Wiltshire, etc. 15-20th c.
FENTON, COLIN. 'The Evelyn family in Wiltshire', *W.A.M.* 58(209), 1961, 18-24. 16-18th c. Includes folded pedigree.
SCULL, G.D. 'Funeral of George Evelyn, West Dean, Wilts', *M.G.H.* 2nd series 1, 1886, 67-8. 1636; includes list of servants and gentlemen mourners.
'Genealogical memoranda relating to the family of Evelyn', *M.G.H.* 2nd series 1, 1886, 1-2, 82-3, 100, 152-6, 176-7, 210, 222-3, 229-34, 258-9, 296-7, 319-22, 332 & 352-6; 2, 1888, 8-11, 24-5, 38-9, 135-8, 184-6, 229, 245, 312 & 327-8; 3, 1890, 242-5, 267-8, 269-71 & 298-300. Surrey, Wiltshire and Hampshire. Includes pedigrees, 16-18th c., monumental inscriptions, parish register extracts, marriage licences, etc.

Eyre
BAILEY, ROSALIE FELLOWS. *New England heritage of Rousmaniere, Ayer, Farwell, and Bourne families.* New York: [ ], 1960. Descended from the Eyre family of Wiltshire.
GANTZ, IDA. *Signpost to Eyrecourt: portrait of the Eyre family triumphant in the cause of liberty, Derbyshire, Wiltshire, Galway, c.1415-1856.* Bath: Kingsmead, 1975. Includes pedigree.
HARTIGAN, A.S. 'Eyre of Wilts', *W.N.Q.* 4, 1902-4, 506-8 & 562-6; 5, 1905-7, 27-31, 49-57, 97-104, 148-53, 218-22, 272-7, 309-13, 346-8, 416-21 & 468-72. See also 5, 1905-7, 426; 6, 1908-10, 189; and 7, 1911-13, 421-2. 16-20th c.
RICHARDSON, MARY E.F. *A history of the Wiltshire family of Eyre.* Mitchell & Hughes, 1897. Includes pedigree, 12-19th c.

Farwell
See Eyre

Fawconer
BARTLETT, R.G. 'Fawconer of Salisbury', *W.N.Q.* 1, 1893-5, 571. See also 421.
MASKELYNE, ANTHONY S. 'Fawconer of Salisbury', *W.N.Q.* 2, 1896-8, 29-33 & 75-9. 17-18th c.

Flower
BARTLETT, R.G. 'Flower, North Wilts', *W.N.Q.* 1, 1893-5, 571-2. Brief extracts from 17th c. parish registers.
S[TORY]-M[ASKELYNE], A.ST.J. 'Memoranda relating to the ancient Wiltshire family of Flower', *W.N.Q.* 8, 1914-16, 167-79 & 301-8. 16th c., includes brief pedigree.

Foster

WARD, JOHN. 'Foster of Marlborough', *W.A.M.*
3(8), 1857, 244-5. Includes folded pedigree, 17-
19th c.
See also Hawkes

Fox

CLAY, CHRISTOPHER. *Public finance and private
wealth: the career of Sir Stephen Fox, 1627-
1716*. Oxford: Clarendon Press, 1978. Includes
pedigrees, 17-18th c.

GANDELL, H.L. 'The Holland baronies', *Coat of
arms* 10, 1969, 276. Fox family of Wiltshire,
18th c.

NORGATE, MARTIN. 'Edward and James Fox,
pipemakers of Trowbridge', *W.A.M.* 78, 1983,
128-9. 17th c.

Francome

'The Francome family', *W.N.Q.* 4, 1902-4, 29-34.
16-18th c.

Fuidge

SCHOMBERG, ARTHUR. 'Bible entries', *M.G.H.* 3rd
series 2, 1898, 194. Relating to the Fuidge and
Gardiner families of Marlborough and Bath,
Somerset, 18-19th c.

Gale

GALE, FRED R. 'Gale of Bolehyde, Co.Wilts',
Notes & queries 170, 1936, 292-4, 312-4 &
331-2. 13-18th c.

Gardiner

See Chivers, Fuidge and Hastings

Garrard

S., J. 'Crawlboys', *W.N.Q.* 7, 1911-13, 32-4.
Garrard family, 18th c.

Gerle

See Dyer

Gernon

See Gresley

Giffard

FANE, ARTHUR. 'Brief notice of the family of
Giffard of Boyton', *W.A.M.* 3(4), 1855, 100-
108. Medieval.

RICHARDSON, DOUGLAS. 'Boyton: the church, the
Giffards, and their successors', *Hatcher review*
1(9), 1980, 26-33. Medieval Giffard family.

Glanville

GLANVILLE-RICHARDS, WM. URMSTON S. *Records of
the Anglo-Norman house of Glanville from A.D.
1050 to 1880*. Mitchell & Hughes, 1882. Of
Yorkshire, Devon, Cornwall, Wiltshire, etc.,
includes pedigrees, 10-19th c.

Goddard

GODDARD, R.W.K. 'Goddard of Englesham: a New
England branch', *W.N.Q.* 3, 1899-1901, 481-96.
17-19th c.

HARMS, JOHN W., & HARMS, PEAR GODDARD. *The
Goddard book*. 2 vols. Baltimore: Gateway
Press, 1984-90. Goddard family of North
Wiltshire and the U.S.A., etc., 16-20th c.
Includes pedigrees.

Family Histories continued

JEFFERIES, RICHARD. *A memoir of the Goddards of
North Wilts, compiled from ancient records,
registers and family papers*. Swindon: Goddard
Association, 1987. Originally published 1873.
Medieval-19th c.

KNAPP, KENNETH NORTHCOT. 'Goddard of
Swindon', *Swindon review* 2, 1946, 7-9.
See also Harington

Godolphin

DIMONT, ELISABETH. *Godolphin family portraits
1610-1781*. Salisbury: Jill Bullen, 1987.

MARSH, F.G. *The Godolphins*. [ ]: privately printed,
1930. Medieval-19th c. Cornwall, Wiltshire,
etc. Includes folded pedigree.

Goldesborough

BENETT-STANFORD, J.M.F. 'Families of East
Knoyle', *W.A.M.* 51(185), 1946, 386-404.
Notes on Goldesborough, Still, Mervyn,
Hunton, Brethers, and Toope, mostly with
pedigrees.

GOLDSBROUGH, ALBERT. *Memorials of the
Goldesborough family*. Cheltenham: E.J.
Burrow & Co., 1930. Originally of Yorkshire,
but of Wiltshire, Somerset, Dorset, and various
other counties from the 15th c.

Goldstone

H[AMMOND], J.J. 'Goldstone of Alderbury',
W.N.Q. 7, 1911-13, 322-5. 17th c.

Goldwyer

BAYLEY, A.R. 'Goldwyer of Somerford Grange and
Salisbury Close', *Genealogists magazine* 7(9),
1937, 455-9. Somerford Grange, Hampshire.
16-19th c.

Family Histories continued

Goodenough
LIGHT, MARY. 'The Goodenoughs of Sherston', *W.N.Q.* **3**, 1899-1901, 385-403. 17-18th c., Sherston Magna.

Gray
WHITTON, DONALD C. *The Grays of Salisbury: an artist family of nineteenth century England.* San Francisco: East Wind Printers, 1976.

Green
See Mortimer

Gresham
See De Boteville

Gresley
CARTER, WILLIAM F. 'Gresley and Gernon', *Genealogist* N.S. **35**, 1919, 176-7. 15th c.

Greve
See De Boteville

Grove
HAWKINS, DESMOND. 'Grove of Ferne House, Wilts', *Notes & queries for Somerset & Dorset* **31**, 1980-85, 120-22. 15-16th c.

Hadrill
MUNROE, MAVIS. 'Hadriel? Hatherell? Hadrell? Hadrill?', *W.F.H.S.* **6**, 1982, 23-5. 19th c.

Harington
POYNTON, F.J. 'Pedigrees showing the connection of Harington of Kelston, Somerset, with the Wiltshire families of Digges, Thorner, Goddard and White', *M.G.H.* 2nd series **5**, 1886, 37-40. 17th c.
For other works on the Harington family, see the Somerset volume of the *British genealogical bibliographies* series.

Harris
MALMESBURY, EARL OF. 'Some anecdotes of the Harris family', *Ancestor* **1**, 1902, 1-27. 17-18th c.

Hastings
LARKEN, GEOFFREY. 'The unknown cousin: Warren Hastings and Barbara Gardiner', *W.A.M.* **72/3**, 1980, 107-118. Includes pedigree showing relationship of Hastings and Gardiner, 17-18th c.

Hawkes
'Hawkes-Foster', *Genealogical quarterly* **41**, 1974-5, 107. Wiltshire families; pedigree, 18th c.

Haynes
See De Boteville

Heard
FULLER, JOHN FRANKLIN. 'Pedigree of Heard, formerly of Wilts, now of Co.Cork', *M.G.H.* 2nd series **4**, 1892, 209-14. 17-19th c.

Heberden
'Heberden pedigree', *Cricklade Historical Society bulletin* **10**, 1975, 5. 19-20th c.

Hector
See De Boteville

Hedges
See Lacy

Herbert
LEVER, TRESHAM. *The Herberts of Wilton.* John Murray, 1967. Includes pedigree, 16-20th c.

Higgons
See De Boteville

Hill
HILL, T.S. 'Pedigree of the family of Hill', *M.G.H.* 2nd series **4**, 1892, 266-70. 17-19th c.

Hinder
HODSDON, JAMES. *The Hinders of Minety and their descendants, 1840-1979.* Cheltenham: the author, 1979.

Hiscock
NOBLE, LEN. *Village folk: the Hiscocks: a Ramsbury family: experiments in oral history.* Locale series **4**. Trowbridge: Wiltshire County Council Library & Museum Service, 1990. 19-20th c.

Hoare
WOODBRIDGE, KENNETH. *Landscape and antiquity: aspects of English culture at Stourhead, 1718 to 1838.* Oxford: Clarendon Press, 1970. In part, a history of the Hoare family.

Hooper
H., R.P. 'Extracts from the registers of Salisbury Cathedral relating to the family of Hooper, of New Sarum and Boveridge', *Genealogist* N.S. **2**, 1885, 42. 16-17th c.

Horsey
WEBB, PETER. 'John Horsey of Martin and his kinsmen at the time of the dissolution of the monasteries: the triumphs and tribulations of a West Country family in the 1530s and 1540s', *Hatcher review* **3**(21), 1986, 10-22. Includes 15-16th c. pedigrees.

Houlton

BOUCHER, R. 'Genealogical notes on the Houlton family', *W.N.Q.* **6**, 83-5, 110-13, 167-70, 211-13 & 270-72. 16-19th c., wills, etc., with pedigree, 17-18th c.

Howell

NORGATE, MARTIN. 'George Howell, pipemaker, of Warminster', *W.A.M.* **79**, 1984, 243. 17-18th c.

Huddesfield

See Rogers

Hungerford

DAVIS, E.L. *Is your name Hungerford? A short history of the famous Hungerford family, with references to the town of Hungerford in Berkshire and the township of Hungerford in Queensland, Australia.* Hungerford: the author, 1984. Berkshire, Wiltshire and Australia, 15-20th c.

FLETCHER, J.M.J. *The Hungerfords and their memorials, past and present: two lectures ...* Salisbury: Bennett Bros., [1936]. Medieval.

HOARE, SIR RICHARD COLT. *Hungerfordiana, or, memoirs of the family of Hungerford.* [ ]: J. & R. Hungerford, 1981. Originally published Shaftesbury: Typis Rutterianis, 1823. Medieval-18th c.

JACKSON, J.E. 'On the Hungerford chapels in Salisbury Cathedral', *W.A.M.* **2**(4), 1855, 83-99. Includes notes on medieval family.

W., J. 'Extracts from the registers of Welford, Berks., and Hungerford and Bedwyn Parva, Wilts., chiefly relating to the family of Hungerford', *Collectanea topographica et genealogica* **5**, 1838, 359-62.

Hunt

ATKINSON, D.R. 'Jeffry Hunt pipes', *W.A.M.* **66**, 1971, 156-61. Hunt family of pipemakers, 17th c.

Huntley

HUNTLEY, GORDON. 'The Huntley and Penny families of Wiltshire and Monmouthshire', *W.F.H.S.* **5**, 1982, 22-3.

Hunton

See Goldesborough

Hurll

WORDSWORTH, CHR. 'The conversion of Mary Hurll, lace-maker's apprentice at Marlborough, 1675 with her indentures, 21 June, 1671', *W.A.M.* **35**(107), 1907, 103-13. Includes apprenticeship indentures.

Hutchins

BOWER, H.B. 'Giles Hutchins, gent., M.P. for Salisbury', *M.G.H.* 5th series **7**, 1929-31, 284. 16-17th c.

Hyde

HAMMOND, J.J. 'Notes on the Hydes of Wilts and Cheshire', *W.N.Q.* **6**, 1908-10, 337-44, 385-90, 433-7 & 498-503; **7**, 1911-13, 116-7 & 377-80. See also **7**, 1911-13, 41-2, 96 & 160-61. Includes folded pedigree, 15-18th c.

JONES, W.H. 'Lord Clarendon and his Trowbridge ancestry', *W.A.M.* **9**(27), 1862, 282-90. Includes pedigree of Hyde and Langford, 16-17th c.

'The Hyde family and Trowbridge', *W.N.Q.* **1**, 1893-5, 156-9. See also 234. 17-18th c.

Ivie

'Ivie family', *W.N.Q.* **8**, 1914-16, 286. Extracts from Malmesbury parish registers, 17th c.

Jacob

'Grant of arms to Tho. Jacob, of Wootton-Bassett, 24 June 1633', *W.N.Q.* **2**, 1896-8, 234-5.

Jaques

'[Jaques family]', *W.N.Q.* **1**, 1893-5, 323-4. See also 130 & 529. 17-19th c.

Jason

MANLEY, F.H. 'Notes of the family of Jason of Broad Somerford', *W.N.Q.* **7**, 1911-13, 181-4, 241-5, 291-8, 361-5, 396-403 & 457-60. 16-18th c. Includes wills and pedigree, etc.

Jenner

FYNMORE, R.J. 'Jenner of Gloucestershire and Wiltshire', *Gloucestershire notes & queries* **10**, 1914, 49-59. Includes pedigree, 18-19th c.

Jordan

See Mortimer

Kent

'Kent of Boscombe', *W.N.Q.* **6**, 1908-10, 431, and **7**, 1911-13, 228-35. See also **6**, 1908-10, 238 & 431-2. 17th c., includes wills.

Kingston

See Lisle

Kipling

JACKSON, RALPH. 'The Lockwood Kiplings at Tisbury, Wiltshire', *Hatcher review* **2**(16), 1983, 278-84. 19th c.

Kirch

See Rudman

Family Histories continued

Knevett
L., C.E. 'Funeral certificate of Sir Henry Knevett and his lady', *Topographer and genealogist* 1, 1846, 469-73. 1598.

Knight
See Nicholas

Knipe
WILLIAMS, J. ANTHONY. 'The decline of a recusant family: the Knipes of Semley', *W.A.M.* 59, 1964, 170-80. See also *ECA journal* 2 (4), 1987, 79-86. 17-19th c.

Lacy
CRAIG, ALGERNON TUDOR. 'Pedigree of Lacy alias Hedges of Alderton, Wilts', *M.G.H.* 5th series 2, 1916-17, 84-9. 16-19th c.

Lake
See De Boteville

Langford
OLIVER, V.L. 'Langford of Trowbridge, Co.Wilts', *W.N.Q.* 3, 1899-1901, 426-7. Extracts from parish register, 16-17th c.
'Langford family', *W.N.Q.* 1, 1893-5, 166. Brief note, 14-18th c.
See also Hyde

Lea
LEA, JAMES HENRY, & LEA, GEORGE HENRY. *The ancestry and posterity of John Lea, of Christian Malford, Wiltshire, and of Pennsylvania in America, 1503-1906.* Philadelphia: Lea Bros., 1906.

Leighton
See De Boteville

Lisle
ROGERS, W.H. HAMILTON. 'Lisle-Kingston-Lisle, of Wodeton, Isle of Wight, Thruxton, Hants and of Wilts and Dorset', in his *Archaeological papers relating to the counties of Somerset, Wilts, Hants and Devon.* [ ]: the author, 1902.

Lloyd
SLEE, JOHN. 'Seven generations of the Lloyd family of masons', *Commemorative art* 34, 1967, 147-9. Of Great Bedwyn.

Long
CHITTY, WALTER. *Historical account of the family of Long of Wiltshire.* Gilbert and Rivington, 1889. Includes pedigree, 17-19th c.

Long continued

'Long of Semington, Whaddon, Monkton, &c., Co.Wilts; Beckington, Stratton, and Downside, Co.Somerset', *M.G.H.* N.S. 3, 1880, 70(f). 16-18th c.
'Pedigree of the Longs of Semington: Rood Ashton and Preshaw branches', *M.G.H.* N.S. 2, 1880, 46(f). Preshaw, Hampshire; 16-19th c.

Longuespee
QUIRQ, ROGER. 'The Longuespee family', *Friends of Salisbury Cathedral* 17, 1947, 11. Medieval.

Ludlow
BAYNE, WILLIAM WILFRID. 'The Ludlows of Hill Deverill', *Virginia magazine of history and biography* 54(3), 1946, 255-7.
'Certified pedigree of Ludlow, of Hill Deverill, Co.Wilts', *W.A.M.* 26(77), 1892, 173. Folded pedigree, 15-19th c.
Pedigree of Ludlow of Hill Deverill, Co.Wilts. Privately printed, [1897].

Mabbutt
See Merryweather

Maffey
DAVIS, F.N. 'Maffey family', *Notes & queries for Somerset & Dorset* 18, 1926, 233-5. Of Dorset and Wiltshire, 18-19th c.

Marsh
PARKER, ALEC MORGAN. *A Marsh family from Wiltshire.* Melbourne: Universal Multiowners, 1979. 16-20th c., primarily a biographical dictionary of Marsh and related families.

Masling
GREENFIELD, BENJ. W. 'Extracts from the parish register of Wootton Bassett, taken October 1842', *M.G.H.* N.S. 1, 1874, 119-20. Mainly concerns Masling or Masklin family, 16-18th c.

Mason
'Funeral certificate: Edmond Mason, D.D., Dean of Salisbury', *M.G.H.* 2nd series 1, 1886, 310.

Massy-Dawson
Massy-Dawson and Poore pedigrees. Frome: Selwood Printing Works, 1937. 18-20th c., pedigrees, with biographical notes, on many associated families.

Matthews
MATTHEWS, GRAHAM. *The Matthews and Knapp families of West Wiltshire.* Coventry: the author, 1987. 18-19th c.

Family Histories *continued*

Maurice
MAURICE, DICK. 'Six generations in Wiltshire', *W.F.H.S.* **8**, 1982, 14-18. Maurice family, 18-20th c., includes pedigree.

Mayell
MAYELL, F.L. *In search of ancestors*. Research Publishing, 1975. Account of the author's experience researching the Mayell family.

Mayo
MAYO, C.H. *A genealogical account of the Mayo and Elton families of Wilts and Hereford and some other adjoining counties, to which are added many genealogies ... of families allied by marriage to the family of Mayo, and a history of the manors of Andrewes and Le Mote, in Cheshunt, Hertfordshire*. 2nd ed. Chiswick Press, 1908. Mayo of Wiltshire, Dorset, Gloucestershire and Herefordshire; Elton of Herefordshire.

Merewether
See Townsend

Merryweather
MERRYWEATHER, ALAN. *Merryweather of Mere and Sedgehill, Wiltshire: a family history, with notes on the families of Amiel, Chandler, Cullimore, Mabbett, Sanderson, Welsh and others*. 2nd ed. Bussage: the author, 1989.

Mervyn
DRAKE, SIR WILLIAM RICHARD. *Fasciculus Mervinensis, being notes historical, genealogical and heraldic of the family of Mervyn*. Privately printed, 1873. Includes pedigrees, 16-19th c. Wiltshire, Sussex and Devon, etc.

VAVASOUR, SIR HENRY MERVYN. 'Mervyn', *M.G.H.* **1**, 1868, 289-91. Funeral certificate of Sir John Mervyn, 1566.

'Tabular pedigree of the Fountel-Gifford branch of the Mervyn family', *M.G.H.* N.S. **1**, 1874, 358-65. Fonthill Gifford. 16th c., includes inquisitions post mortem and wills.

'Tabular pedigree of the Pertwood branch of the Mervyn family', *M.G.H.* N.S. **2**, 1877, 3-11. 15-19th c.

See also Goldesborough

Montacute
KITE, ed. 'Some notes on the Montacutes, Earls of Salisbury', *W.N.Q.* **4**, 1902-4, 481-93 & 529-43. Medieval; includes pedigree, etc.

Montagu
CUNNINGTON, WILLIAM. 'Memoir of George Montagu', *W.A.M.* **3**(7), 1857, 87-94. Includes folded pedigree of Montagu of Lackham, 17-19th c.

Montgomery
See De Boteville

Morres
ADDISON, W.G. 'Three Wiltshire parsons', *Theology* **54**, 1951, 329-35. Robert Morres, R.H. Hill, and A.P. Morres, vicars of Britford.

Morse
SADLER, J. 'Morse, of Rodbourne Cheney, etc.', *W.N.Q.* **6**, 1908-10, 361-4, 503-7 & 562-5. See also **7**, 1911-13, 46-7. 16-18th c.

Mortimer
BAUMAN, JOHN ANDREW, et al. *The ancestry and descendants of James Mortimer (1842-1917) of Logan, Cache County, Utah, including descendants of the Jordan, Green, Mortimer and Sheppard families of Great Faringdon, Berkshire, and Liddington, Wiltshire, England*. Bismarck, North Dakota: Beth Bauman, 1986. 17-20th c.

Moule
LEWIS, R.W.M. *The family of Moule of Melksham, Fordington, and Melbourne*. [ ]: privately printed, 1938. 18-20th c.

Naish
SLATTER, DOREEN, ed. *The diary of Thomas Naish*. W.R.S. **20**, 1965. Includes short account of the Naish family, 18th c.

Neville
HICKS, M.A. 'The Neville Earldom of Salisbury, 1429-71', *W.A.M.* **72/3**, 1980, 141-7.

Nicholas
KITE, ed. 'Judge Nicholas: his parentage and birthplace', *W.N.Q.* **3**, 505-10 & 539-46. Includes pedigree, 15-17th c.

K[ITE], E., & S[CHOMBERG], A. 'Nicholas and Knight', *W.N.Q.* **8**, 1914-16, 374-8. Marriage settlement, 1670.

SCHOMBERG, A. 'Judge Nicholas', *W.N.Q.* **5**, 385-91. Includes marriage settlement and probate inventory, 17th c.

Genealogical memoranda relating to the family of Nicholas. Hounslow: J. Gotelee, 1874. Medieval-19th c.

Noad
See Westall

Family Histories continued

Nott
'Pedigree of Nott of London and Braydon, Wilts',
M.G.H. N.S. 3, 1880, 233-5.

Noyes
WARD, J. 'Noyes', *W.A.M.* 3(9), 1857, 380. Brief
note, 16-17th c.
'John Noyes of Calne', *W.N.Q.* 4, 1902-4, 365-71,
420-24 & 461-4. Includes 17th c. pedigree.

Packer
PACKER, DONNA SMITH. *On footings from the past:
the Packers in England.* U.S.A.: [the author],
1988. Gloucestershire, Westminster, Wiltshire
and U.S.A.; 15-18th c. Includes a good
bibliography.

Painter
c. 'Name 'Painter' in and near North Wilts',
W.N.Q. 4, 1902-4, 80-88 & 121-4. 16-18th c.

Paradise
KITE, EDWARD, & SCHOMBERG, ARTHUR. 'Family of
Paradise', *Genealogist* N.S. 37, 1921, 74-84 &
151-4. 16-18th c., includes wills.
'Paradise family', *W.N.Q.* 7, 1914-16, 49-58.
Includes pedigree, 16-18th c., monumental
inscriptions, parish register extracts, etc.

Parry
See Westall

Pelling
'Pelling family', *W.N.Q.* 6, 1908-10, 459-63. 16-
17th c.

Peniston
COWAN, MICHAEL. 'The Penistons: a Salisbury
family of Catholic architects and yeomen, 1770-
1911', *W.A.M.* 80, 1986, 184-91. Includes
pedigree.

Penn
HOGG, O.F.G. 'Pedigree of Penn of Co.Wilts and of
Bristol', *W.A.M.* 60, 1965, 130(f). Folded; 16-
17th c.
HOGG, OLIVER F.G. *Further light on the ancestry of
William Penn.* Society of Genealogists, 1964.
Buckinghamshire, Hertfordshire, Shropshire,
Wiltshire and Gloucestershire; includes
pedigrees, 12-18th c.
'Penn of Rodbourne', *W.N.Q.* 7, 1911-13, 158-60.
17th c.

Penruddock
NOBLE, ARTHUR H. *The Penruddock family: the
genealogical & historical account of the
Penruddock families of Cumberland and
Wiltshire, with a pedigree of 17 generations
from about 1400 to present day.* [ ]: A.H. Noble,
1968. Duplicated typescript.

Penny
See Huntley

Perrett
PERRETT, GEORGE EDWARD. *In search of the
Perretts: a family history and genealogical
survey.* Crowborough, Sussex: the author,
[1983]. 16-19th c.
The Perrett Society journal 1984-

Phillipps
P[HILLIPPS], T. *Collectanea de familiis diversis,
quibus nomen est Phillipps, praesertim vero de
illis apud Wanborough in Com.Wilton, et quid
Broadway in Com.Wigorn.* [Middle Hill]: Typis
Medio Montaris, [1840?]. Includes many wills,
deeds, pedigrees, etc.; medieval-19th c.

Pillinger
LINDEGAARD, PATRICIA. 'Wiltshire wanderings',
W.F.H.S. 1, 1981, 24-6. Pillinger family, 17-
18th c.

Pitman
PITMAN, H.A. 'Pitman of Quarley and North
Tidworth', *M.G.H.* 5th series 6, 1926-8, 72-8.
Quarley, Hampshire.

Pole
DORLING, E.E. 'Notes on the arms of Cardinal
Pole', *W.A.M.* 30(92), 1899, 338-47. Includes
pedigree, 12-16th c.

Poole
DUNLOP, J. RENTON. 'Pedigree of the Pooles of
Sapperton and Coates, Gloucestershire, and of
Poole and Chelworth, Wiltshire', *M.G.H.* 5th
series 3, 1918-19, 205-11. 16-17th c.
'Pedigree of the Pooles of Poole, Chelworth,
Oaksey and Kemble, Wiltshire', *M.G.H.* 5th
series 3, 1918-19, 212-5. 16-18th c.
'Wiltshire members of the Long Parliament',
W.N.Q. 1, 1893-5, 329-34. Despite the title,
concerns the Poole family of Oaksey, 16-17th c.

Poore
JONES, W.H. 'On the surname Poore: its origin and
meaning', *W.A.M.* 19(56), 1881, 232-4.
Medieval.

Popham
See Calston

Pote
See Rudman

Powell
POWELL, EDGAR. *The pedigree of the family of Powell, sometime resident at Mildenhall, Barton Mills, and Hawstead in Co.Suffolk, and afterwards at Homerton and Clapton, Co.Middlesex, and elsewhere, from Henry VII to Victoria, to which are added pedigrees of Thistlethwayte of Co.Wilts.* The author, 1891.

Prater
PRATHER, JOHN WILLIAM. *Praters in Wiltshire, 1480-1670.* Hendersonville, N.S.: [the author?], 1987. Includes extracts from parish registers, wills, deeds, etc.

Raleigh
H[AMMOND], J.J. 'Raleigh of Downton, Wilts', *W.N.Q.* **7**, 1911-13, 332-3. Heraldry.
PINK, W.D. 'Raleigh of Downton', *W.N.Q.* **2**, 1896-8, 90-91. See also **5**, 1905-7, 574-5.

Redman
O'GRADY, CLODAGH. *The Redmans of Halfway House.* Ramsbury: the author, 1978. Includes pedigrees, 18-20th c.

Reeves
See Whitaker

Richmond
RICHMOND, HENRY I. *Richmond family records.* 3 vols. Adlard & Sons, 1933-38. v.1. Maryland, Virginia, New England, Ireland and Somerset. v.2. The Richmonds alias Webb of Wiltshire. v.3. The Richmonds of Wiltshire. 15-20th c. 'Pedigree of Richmond alias Webb, of Draycott Folliot, Wilts', *M.G.H.* 5th series **7**, 1929-31, 41-9. 17-19th c.

Rivers
See Savage

Robins
ROBBINS, MILLS R. *Gleanings of the Robins or Robbins family of England ...* 2nd ed. Devizes: C.H. Woodward, 1908. 13-20th c., includes pedigrees.

Rogers
ROGERS, W.H. HAMILTON. 'Rogers-Courtenay-Huddesfield of Bradford-on-Avon, Wilts, Cannington, Somerset, and Shillingford, Dorset', in his *Archaeological papers relating to the counties of Somerset, Wilts, Hants and Devon.* [ ]: the author, 1902.

ROGERS, W.H.H. 'Rogers-Courtenay-Huddesfield of Bradford-on-Avon, Wilts, Cannington, Somerset, and Shillingford, Devon', *W.N.Q.* **3**, 1899-1901, 337-45. 16th c.

Rolf
FORSYTH, C.L. *John Rolf and his descendants.* Melbourne: the author, 1984. Wiltshire and Australia; 18-20th c.
See also Dyer

Rousmaniere
See Eyre

Rudman
MELVILLE, JANET. *Rudman register and related families: Erasmus, Pote, Kirch.* Port Elizabeth, Western Australia: the author, 1980. 19-20th c. Wiltshire and Australia, etc.

Sadler
EVERETT, C.R. 'Notes on the prebendal mansion of Sherborne Monastery, commonly known as the King's House, in the Close of Sarum', *W.A.M.* **47**(164), 1936, 398-405. Includes notes on Sadler and Beach families.
'Wroughton registers: Sadler', *W.N.Q.* **5**, 1905-7, 570-73. 17-18th c. births and baptisms.

Salisbury
See Neville

Samborne
SAMBORN, V.S. 'A possible Samborne ancestry', *Ancestor* **11**, 1904, 61-70. Of Wiltshire, Somerset and Berkshire; 12-15th c.
SANBORN, V.C. *Genealogy of the family of Samborne or Sanborn in England and America, 1194-1898.* 2 pts. Concord: privately printed, 1899. Of Wiltshire, Berkshire, Hampshire, Somerset and America. Includes pedigrees.
SANBORNE, V.C. 'The Samborne ancestry', *Genealogist* N.S. **13**, 1897, 145-52. See also **14**, 1898, 72, & **15**, 1899, 264. Medieval.
'Samborne family', *W.N.Q.* **1**, 1893-5, 373-4. See also 564-5, and **2**, 1896-8, 43-5 & 92-3. 13-14th c.

Sanderson
See Merryweather

Saunders
EVANS, G.E. *Pastoral pedigree.* Privately published, 1977. Saunders family, 18-20th c.

Savage
HORTON-SMITH, L.G.H. 'The family of Savage of Burbage Savage, Co.Wilts', *Notes & queries* **188**, 1945, 233-4. 13-16th c.

Family Histories continued

Savage *continued*

HORTON-SMITH, L.GRAHAM H. *The family of Savage of Co.Wilts, with a passing note on the dormant Earldom of Rivers*. Devizes: C.H. Woodward, 1944.

Scammell

SCAMMELL, A.J. 'Ancient family rediscovered', *Greenwood tree* 7(2), 1982, 35-6. Scammell family of Tisbury.

Schneider

'Schneider of North Wraxhall', *W.N.Q.* 5, 1905-7, 384. Pedigree, 18-19th c.

Seede

'Seede of Tetbury, Upton Cheyney, Bitton, Bisley, Rodborough, Stroud and Bristol, Gloucestershire, and of Castlecombe, Wiltshire', *M.G.H.* 3rd series 4, 1892, 7-11. 16-18th c.

Selfe

HEATHCOTE, T.G.J. 'Place House, Melksham with some account of the Selfe family', *W.N.Q.* 4, 1902-4, 193-201. 17th c., includes monumental inscriptions.

HEATHCOTE, T.G.J. 'Thomas Selfe, of Cadley, in Melksham', *W.N.Q.* 4, 1902-4, 349-56. Includes will of Isaac Selfe of Melksham, 1741.

Sewster

ANDREWS, HERBERT C. 'The Sewster family of Godmanchester, Hunts., Steeple Morden, Cambs., and Ashwell, Herts., with notes on the Dodington family of Wilts and Herts.', *M.G.H.* 5th series 7, 1929-31, 333-48. Includes pedigrees, medieval-17th c.

Seymour

BARTLETT, R.G. 'Seymour in Rollestone registers', *W.N.Q.* 2, 1896-8, 533. See also 586-9.

JACKSON, J.E. *Wulfhall and the Seymours, with an appendix of original documents discovered at Longleat*. [ ]: privately printed, 1874. Reprinted from *W.A.M.* 15(44), 1875, 140-207. 16-17th c., includes appendix calendaring 26 documents, which give many names of household members.

LOCKE, A. AUDREY. *The Seymour family: history and romance*. Constable & Co., 1911.

ST.MAUR, H. *Annals of the Seymours, being a history of the Seymour family from early times to within a few years of the present*. Kegan Paul Trench Trubner & Co., 1902.

Sharington

VERNON, THELMA E. 'Inventory of Sir Henry Sharington: contents of Lacock House, 1575', *W.A.M.* 62, 1967, 72-82. Includes notes on family. Not a probate inventory.

Sheppard

See Mortimer

Silverthorn

REED, FRANK FREMONT. *History of the Silverthorn family*. Chicago: Silverthorn(e) Family Association, 1982. Continued in *Silverthorn(e) family newsletter* 1984-. Steeple Ashton and U.S.A., 16-20th c. Includes many transcripts of original sources.

Skutt

'Grant of arms to John Skutt, 1546', *W.N.Q.* 5, 1905-7, 421-4.

Smallbone

GEORGE, BRIAN. 'Genealogical agony', *W.F.H.S.* 7, 1982, 4-6. Smallbone family, 19-20th c.

GEORGE, BRIAN. 'The Smallbones discovered, or, if at first you don't succeed ...', *W.F.H.S.* 20, 1985, 13-15. 19-20th c.

GEORGE, BRIAN. 'More Smallbones discovered', *W.F.H.S.* 35, 1989, 27-8. Berkshire, Hampshire and Wiltshire, 17-19th c.

Smith

P., T. 'Smith family', *W.N.Q.* 1, 1893-5, 374-5. See also 425-6. 17th c.

'Two informative bibles', *W.F.H.S.* 31, 1988, 31. Births, marriages and deaths of Smith of Salisbury, and Ellison. 19-20th c.

Snigg

'Snigg', *W.N.Q.* 5, 1905-7, 145-8. See also 330. Includes will of Sir George Snygge, 1617.

South

H., J.J. *Thomas South, of Bossington Hall, Hants'*, W.N.Q. 6, 1908-10, 381-4. See also 326. Includes brief pedigree of South of Salisbury, 16th c.

S[TORY]-M[ASKELYNE], A.ST.J. 'The family of South', *W.N.Q.* 7, 1911-13, 9-15, 51-7 & 214-17. 15-16th c., includes pedigrees.

Speke

MURDOCH, SOPHIA. *Record of the Speke family (Jordans, Somerset)*. Reading: H.T. Morley, [1900]. Of Somerset, Devon, Yorkshire, Lancashire, Wiltshire and Berkshire.

28

Stafford

KITE, EDWARD. 'John Stafford, Archbishop of Canterbury, and his Wiltshire parentage', *W.N.Q.* 2, 1896-8, 218-22 & 255-61. See also 298-301, 438-9 & 488-91. Includes folded pedigree, 15th c., with monumental inscription.

PINK, W.D. 'Stafford of Southwick, Grafton and Blatherwick', *Genealogist* N.S. 31, 1915, 173-8. Southwick, Wiltshire; Grafton, Worcestershire; Blatherwick, Northamptonshire. 14-15th c.

ROGERS, W.H.H. 'Stafford family of Suthwyke in North Bradley, Wilts., and Hoke, Dorset', *W.N.Q.* 3, 1899-1901, 193-202. See also 4, 1902-4, 45. Reprinted in his *Archaeological papers relating to the counties of Somerset, Wilts, Hants and Devon*. [ ]: the author, 1902. Includes pedigree, 14-15th c.

Stevens

'John Steevens', *W.N.Q.* 8, 1914-16, 236-7. See also 192. Lists many Stevens baptisms at Manningford Bruce, 16th c.

Still

See Goldesborough

Stokes

SCHOMBERG, ARTHUR. *Some notes on the Stokes family, (Cos. of Wilts and Glos)*. Devizes: Gazette Office, 1903.

SCHOMBERG, A. 'Stokes of Seend', *W.N.Q.* 5, 1902-5, 193-8, 240-48, 289-95, 348-53, 391-6, 458-62, 503-10 & 552-61; 6, 1908-10, 4-9, 49-57, 99-107, 171-6, 193-7, 244-8 & 289-302. See also 404-5. Includes monumental inscriptions, extracts from family bible, inquisitions post mortem, wills, chancery proceedings, pedigree, 14-17th c., etc.

S[CHOMBERG], A. 'Stokes', *M.G.H.* N.S. 3, 1880, 309. Extracts from family bible, 17-18th c.

Stourton

MOWBRAY, LORD. *The history of the noble house of Stourton, of Stourton in the county of Wilts ...* 2 vols. Elliot Stock, 1899. Medieval-19th c.

STRATTON, RICHARD FLOWER. *A history of the Wiltshire Strattons*. Castle Cary: Castle Cary Press, 1987. 19-20th c. This supersedes STRATTON, JAMES. *A history of the Wiltshire Strattons*. Winchester: Fred Smith, 1902. See also Brown.

Stumpe

J., J.G. 'Memorials of the family of Stumpe of Malmesbury', *Collectanea topographica et genealogica* 7, 1841, 81-4. Pedigree, 16-17th c.

LEWIS, GORDON. 'A family tree ... Stump', *W.F.H.S.* 32, 1989, 10-12. 16-20th c.

'A Stump pedigree', *W.N.Q.* 8, 1914-16, 369-72. See also 427. 17-19th c.

'William Stumpe of Malmesbury, his descendants and relatives', *W.N.Q.* 8, 1914-16, 385-95, 444-54, 482-7 & 531-7. See also 552. 15-17th c. Includes wills, inquisitions post mortem.

Swinnerton

See Dyer

Sydenham

SYDENHAM, G.F. *The history of the Sydenham family, collected from family documents, pedigrees, deeds, and copious memoranda*. ed. A.T. Cameron. East Molesey: E. Dwelly, 1928. Includes monumental inscriptions, extensive list of wills, many pedigrees, etc., etc.

Thistlethwayte

See Powell

Thorner

See Harington

Thynne

BURNETT, DAVID. *Longleat: the story of an English country house*. Collins, 1978. Thynne family, 16-20th c. Includes pedigree.

ROUND, J.H. 'The origin of the Thynnes', *Genealogist* N.S. 11, 1895, 193-5. Includes pedigree, 15-16th c.

WALL, ALISON D. *Two Elizabethan women: correspondence of Joan and Maria Thynne, 1575-1611*. W.R.S. 38, 1983. See also De Boteville.

Titford

TITFORD, JOHN, et al. *The Titford family, 1547-1947: come wind, come weather*. Phillimore, 1989. Prize-winning study, 17-20th c. Wiltshire, Somerset, London, etc.

TITFORD, JOHN. 'The Titford Family: come wind, come weather', *W.F.H.S.* 29, 1988, 10-13.

Toope

See Goldesborough

Family Histories continued

Townsend
WALEY, M.H. 'James Townsend of Great
Cheverell, 1654-1730, with some notes on his
family in Great Cheverell and Stratford sub
Castle, 1653-1748', *W.A.M.* **60**, 1965, 109-19.
Includes pedigrees of Townsend and
Merewether.

Trenchard
FRY, E.A. 'Trenchard', *W.N.Q.* **4**, 1902-4, 472.
Pedigree, 16-17th c.

Trowbridge
TROWBRIDGE, C.W. *The Trowbridge family history,
1690-1990*. Wantage: Wessex Press, 1991.
Includes pedigrees and many extracts from
parish registers.

Tugwell
BARNES, F.H. *History of a family: Barnes
supplement; no.2*. [ ]: the author, 1972. Includes
pedigree of Tugwell, 16-19th c.

Tyndale
GREENFIELD, B. WYATT. 'Tyndale: extracts from
parish registers, etc.', *M.G.H.* **1**, 1868, 244-5 &
274-5. Of Thornbury and Iron Acton,
Gloucestershire, and Kingston St.Michael,
Wiltshire.

Tyse
SCHOMBERG, ARTHUR. 'Family of Tyse', *W.N.Q.* **7**,
1911-13, 347-53. Probate records, 17th c.

Vilett
'The Society's mss., note 1: the Vilett family',
W.A.M. **30**(91), 1899, 221-9. Includes pedigree,
16-17th c.

Vivash
VIVASH, E.P. 'What's in a name?', *W.F.H.S.* **7**,
1982, 22-3. Vivash family, medieval-17th c.

Walter
JUDD, J.S. 'A Walter family at Winterslow',
W.A.M. **53**(190), 1949, 63-4. Pedigree,
16-17th c.

Walton
'Isaac Walton and his connexion with Wiltshire',
W.N.Q. **4**, 1902-4, 288-94 & 385-93. Includes
wills, 17th c.

Wansbrough
DAWSON, FRANK. 'The Wansbroughs of Wiltshire',
W.F.H.S. **4**, 1981, 17-24. See also **24**, 1987, 10-
14 & **25**, 1987, 32-7. Includes pedigrees,
17-19th c.

Wansey
MANN, J.L. DE 'A Wiltshire family of clothiers:
George and Hester Wansey, 1683-1714',
Economic history review 2nd series **9**(2), 1956,
241-53.

Wapshat
VINCENT, MARTIN. 'The birth and death of a name',
W.F.H.S. **9**, 1983, 14-15. Wapshat family,
17-18th c.

Webb
HAMMOND, JOHN J. 'Webb of Great Canford,
Dorset, and Odstock, Wiltshire', *Notes &
queries for Somerset & Dorset* **10**, 1907,
209-14.
See also Richmond

Welsh
See Merryweather

West
HARGETION, JULIETTE. 'The Wests of Wiltshire',
W.F.H.S. **35**, 1989, 16-18. Includes pedigree,
19-20th c.

Westall
NOAD, L. MICHAEL. *A short history of Noad and
Son, chartered surveyors, ... founded 1820*.
Chippenham: Noad & Son, 1980. Westall, Parry
and Noad families' business.

Whatmore
WHATMORE, A.W. 'Marshwood House, Dinton',
W.N.Q. **1**, 1893-5, 147-9. Whatmore family;
18th c.
WHATMORE, A.W. 'Whatmore of Wilton', *M.G.H.*
2nd series **4**, 1892, 193-4. Pedigree, 18-19th c.,
with wills.
WHATMORE, GEOFFREY. 'The Whatmores of
Wilton', *W.F.H.S.* **13**, 1984, 4-7.

Whitaker
REEVES, MARJORIE. *Sheep bell and plough share:
the story of two village families*. Bradford on
Avon: Moonraker Press, 1978. Reprinted
Granada, 1980. Whitaker and Reeves families
of Bratton; includes pedigrees, 16-20th c.
REEVES, MARJORIE. 'A Wiltshire ancestry',
W.F.H.S. **19**, 1985, 6-9. Whitaker family, 16-
19th c.

White
See Harington

Willoughby
BODDINGTON, REGINALD STUART. 'Pedigree of the
family of Willoughby', *Genealogist* **2**, 1878,
91-4. Of London and Wiltshire; 17th c.

Wyndham

WYNDHAM, H.A. *A family history, 1688-1837: the Wyndhams of Somerset, Sussex and Wiltshire.* Oxford U.P., 1950.

'Entries relating to the Wyndham family ...', *M.G.H.* 2nd series **2**, 1888, 292-4. Extracts from a prayer book, 18th c.

'Memoranda relating to the family of Wyndham of Norrington, of Salisbury, and of Dinton, Co.Wilts., of Hawkchurch, Co.Dorset, of Eversley, Co.Hants, etc., 1609-1753', *M.G.H.* 2nd series **4**, 1892, 36-8, 54-6 & 77-80. From a diary.

Young

YOUNG, W.E.V. 'Notes on the Young family of Ebbesbourne Wake', *W.A.M.* **62**, 1967, 110-14, 16-20th c.

8. PARISH REGISTERS AND OTHER RECORDS OF BIRTHS, MARRIAGES AND DEATHS

The importance of parish registers and other sources of information on births, marriages and deaths cannot be overstated. Wiltshire genealogists are fortunate that many registers—especially marriage registers—have been published. It is nevertheless important that entries found in printed registers should be checked against the original if at all possible. Some parish register editors were exceptionally accurate—but others could produce woeful errors! For a listing of original parish registers, see Carter's *Location of documents for Wiltshire parishes.* (See above, section 2B.)

Nonconformist registers are listed in:

COLEMAN, A. 'Lists of non-parochial registers and records', *W.A.M.* **28**(83), 1895, 149-55.

Wiltshire parishes included in the important Nimrod marriage index are listed in:

'Wiltshire parishes in the Nimrod index of marriages', *Journal of the Bristol & Avon Family History Society,* **11**, 1978, 7. See also **13**, 1978, 11; **15**, 1979, 25; **18**, 1979, 14; & **19**, 1980, 19.

Many Wiltshire men and women 'strayed' into other parts of the country. Surnames in the Wiltshire Family History Society's 'strays index', which is presumably based largely on parish registers, are listed in:

WILSON, PAT. 'Strays index', *W.F.H.S.* **23**, 1987, 11-14; **24**, 1987, 14-20; **25**, 1987, 15-19; **26**, 1987, 30-32. See also **28**, 1988, 20-21; **32**, 1989, 20-21; **36**, 1990, 27-8; **40**, 1991, 16-17.

Wiltshire extracts from a London register are listed in:

'Registers of Somerset House Chapel, 1714-1775', *W.N.Q.* **5**, 1905-7, 372-4.

Wiltshire marriages 'down under' for 1866-7 are listed in:

'Marriages in Victoria', *W.F.H.S.* **39**, 1990, 11; **40**, 1991, 13.

Births, marriages and deaths are frequently recorded in contemporary magazines and newspapers. For some 1779 extracts, see:

GODDARD, RAINALD W.K. 'Old magazine extracts: Wiltshire births, marriages and deaths in the *Town and country magazine* ... for 1779', *W.N.Q.* **1**, 1893-5, 165-6.

Every Wiltshire genealogist should consult the seventeenth century marriage bonds of the Diocese of Salisbury. See:

Parish Registers etc. continued

NEVILL, EDMUND. 'Marriage licences of
Salisbury', *Genealogist* N.S. **24**, 1908, 51-5,
128-33, 188-92 & 276-80; **25**, 1909, 46-52, 94-
9, 167-72 & 235-9; **26**, 1910, 52-5, 113-7, 149-
54 & 232-40; **27**, 1911, 39-47, 96-104, 172-9 &
233-41; **28**, 1912, 51-6, 81-7, 153-60 & 242-9;
29, 1913, 42-8, 118-21, 163-70 & 252-9; **30**,
1914, 50-56, 121-7, 182-7 & 238-46; **31**, 1915,
115-25, 178-88 & 258-68; **32**, 1916, 61-5, 126-
33, 202-8 & 262-72; **33**, 1917, 44-55, 114-26,
198-208 & 261-5, **34**, 1918, 44-8, 103-8, 161-73
& 235-44; **35**, 1919, 56-8, 127-38 & 235-40; **36**,
1920, 43-50, 106-9, 158-63 & 215-9; **37**, 1921,
50-53, 100-106, 162-5 & 210-20. 1615-81.
NEVILL, EDMUND R. 'Peculiars of the Dean and
Chapter of Sarum', *W.N.Q.* **6**, 1908-10, 31-6,
72-81, 121-9, 176-9, 213-24, 255-60, 321-6,
357-61, 395-8, 473-5, 516-8 & 565-6; **7**, 1911-
13, 39-41, 76-8, 119-22, 221-3, 325-9, 353-7,
406-11, 460-5, 516-8 & 540-46; **8**, 1914-16, 28-
31, 78-82, 162-6, 229-34, 378-82, 417-20 &
454-7. Marriage bonds, 17th c. Not completed.
For a discussion of an index to marriage bonds,
1700-1823, see:
WHIPPLE, HAZEL. 'Serendipity in Sarum marriage
bonds', *Oxfordshire Family Historian* **2**(5),
1981, 131-5.

Aldbourne
L., C.E. 'Extracts from the parish register of
Aldbourne, North Wilts., with a few church
notes, and genealogical particulars',
Collectanea topographica et genealogica, **6**,
1840, 385-91.

Alderton
SYMONDS, W. 'Marriages at Alderton, 1606-1812',
in PHILLIMORE, W.P.W., & SADLER, JOHN, eds.
W.P.R.M. **1**, *P.P.R.S.* **57**. Phillimore, 1905, 131-
40.

All Cannings
PARRY, JOSEPH HENRY, ed. *The registers of
Allcannings and Etchilhampton, Wiltshire.*
Devizes: Gazette Printing Works, 1905. All
Cannings, 1577-1812; Etchilhampton, 1630-
1812.

Allington
RUDDLE, C.S., ed. 'Marriages at Allington, 1623 to
1812', in PHILLIMORE, W.P.W., & SADLER, JOHN,
eds. *W.P.R.M.* **3**, *P.P.R.S.* **76**. Phillimore, 1906,
143-6.

Alton Barnes
PARRY, J.H., ed. 'Marriages at Alton Barnes, 1597
to 1812', in PHILLIMORE, W.P.W., & SADLER,
JOHN, eds. *W.P.R.M.* **6**, *P.P.R.S.* **105**.
Phillimore, 1908, 123-7.

Ashley
REDFERN, J. LEMON, ed. 'Marriages at Ashley,
1658 to 1812', in PHILLIMORE, W.P.W., & SADLER,
JOHN, eds. *W.P.R.M.* **3**, *P.P.R.S.* **76**. Phillimore,
1906, 67-72.

Baverstock
GODDARD, C.V., ed. 'Marriages at Baverstock,
1559 to 1812', in PHILLIMORE, W.P.W., NEVILL,
EDMUND, & SADLER, JOHN, eds. *W.P.R.M.* **5**,
P.P.R.S. **99**. Phillimore, 1907, 135-45.

Beechingstoke
WILTSHIRE FAMILY HISTORY SOCIETY, eds. *The
bishop's transcripts and parish registers of
Beechingstoke: baptisms and burials, 1566-
1837.* Devizes: W.F.H.S., 1992.
PARRY, J.H., ed. 'Marriages at Beechingstoke,
1590 to 1812', in PHILLIMORE, W.P.W., & SADLER,
JOHN, eds. *W.P.R.M.* **8**, *P.P.R.S.* **127**.
Phillimore, 1909, 93-103.

Bemerton
See Fugglestone St.Peter

Bishops Canning
PARRY, J.H., ed. *The Registers of Bishops
Cannings, Wiltshire.* Devizes: Gazette Printing
Works, 1906. 1591-1811.

Bishopstone
JAMES, JUNE. ['Names from Bishopstone
baptismal register, 1851-99'] *W.F.H.S.* **15**,
1984, 15-16.

Boscombe
RUDDLE, C.S., ed. 'Marriages at Boscombe, 1625
to 1812', in PHILLIMORE, W.P.W., & SADLER,
JOHN, eds. *W.P.R.M.* **3**, *P.P.R.S.* **76**. Phillimore,
1906, 147-51.

Boyton
HAMMOND, J.J., ed. 'Marriages at Boyton, 1560 to
1837', in PHILLIMORE, W.P.W., & SADLER, JOHN,
eds. *W.P.R.M.* **12**, *P.P.R.S.* **189**. Phillimore,
1912, 93-108.
H[AMMOND], J.J. 'Somerset and Dorset marriages
at Boyton, Wilts', *Notes & queries for Somerset
& Dorset* **12**, 1911, 57-8.

Bratton

GOFTON, J.E., ed. 'Marriages at Bratton, 1542 to 1837', in PHILLIMORE, W.P.W., & SADLER, JOHN, eds. *W.P.R.M.* **12**, *P.P.R.S.* **189**. Phillimore & Co., 1912, 1-28.

Brinkworth

MANLEY, F.H., ed. 'Marriages at Brinkworth, 1653 to 1812', in PHILLIMORE, W.P.W., & SADLER, JOHN, eds. *W.P.R.M.* **10**, *P.P.R.S.* **155**. Phillimore, 1910, 19-43.

Britford

BAKER, T.H. 'Marriages at Britford, 1573 to 1812', in PHILLIMORE, W.P.W., & SADLER, JOHN, eds. *W.P.R.M.* **3**, *P.P.R.S.* **76**. Phillimore, 1906, 1-36.

B[AKER], T.H. 'Notes from Wiltshire registers', *Notes & queries for Somerset & Dorset* **10**, 1907, 33-4. Parish register entries from Britford, Ham, Wylye and Fisherton Anger relating to Somerset and Dorset natives.

Broad Chalke

MOORE, CECIL GURDEN, ed. *Registers of Broad Chalke, Co.Wilts, from 1538 to 1780*. Mitchell & Hughes, 1881.

Bulford

RUDDLE, C.S., ed. 'Marriages at Bulford, 1608 to 1812', in PHILLIMORE, W.P.W., & SADLER, JOHN, eds. *W.P.R.M.* **3**, *P.P.R.S.* **76**. Phillimore, 1906, 129-32.

Burbage

See Collingbourne Ducis

Castle Eaton

LUCKMAN, C.M.R. 'Marriages at Castle Eaton, 1549 to 1812', in PHILLIMORE, W.P.W., & SADLER, JOHN, eds. *W.P.R.M.* **6**, *P.P.R.S.* **105**. Phillimore, 1908, 1-13.

Charlton

FORSTER-BROWN, S., ed. 'Marriages at Charlton, near Pewsey, 1696 to 1812', in PHILLIMORE, W.P.W., & SADLER, JOHN, eds. *W.P.R.M.* **7**, *P.P.R.S.* **119**. Phillimore, 1908, 140-44.

Charlton St.Peter

WILTSHIRE FAMILY HISTORY SOCIETY. *The bishop's transcripts and parish registers of Charlton St.Peter: baptisms, 1611-1837*. Devizes: W.F.H.S., 1992.

Chilton Foliot

W., J. 'Church-notes, and extracts from the parish registers, of Chilton Foliot, Co.Wilts', *Topographer & genealogist* **3**, 1858, 575-91.

Chippenham

HALL, R. VINE. 'Extracts from the parish registers of Chippenham, Wilts', *M.G.H.* 5th series **8**, 1932-4, 173-4.

Chirton

PARRY, J.H. 'Marriages at Cherington alias Chirton, 1588 to 1812', in PHILLIMORE, W.P.W., & SADLER, JOHN, eds. *W.P.R.M.* **6**. *P.P.R.S.* **105**. Phillimore, 1908, 101-15.

Chisledon

WILTSHIRE FAMILY HISTORY SOCIETY, eds. *The bishop's transcripts and parish registers of Chisledon: baptisms, 1605-1837*. Devizes: W.F.H.S., 1992.

WILTSHIRE FAMILY HISTORY SOCIETY, eds. *The bishop's transcripts and parish registers of Chisledon: burials, 1605-1837*. Devizes: W.F.H.S., 1992.

MOULDER, VICTOR J., ed. 'Marriages at Chisledon, 1641 to 1812', in PHILLIMORE, W.P.W., & SADLER, JOHN, eds. *W.P.R.M.* **8**. *P.P.R.S.* **127**. Phillimore, 1909, 1-22.

Cholderton

OWEN, A.E. BRISCO, ed. 'Marriages at Cholderton, 1664 to 1752', in PHILLIMORE, W.P.W., & SADLER, JOHN, eds. *W.P.R.M.* **7**. *P.P.R.S.* **119**. Phillimore, 1908, 95-8.

Christian Malford

MANLEY, F.H., ed. 'Marriages at Christian Malford, 1653 to 1812', in PHILLIMORE, W.P.W., & SADLER, JOHN, eds. *W.P.R.M.* **10**. *P.P.R.S.* **155**. Phillimore, 1910, 45-67.

Chute

W., J. 'Extracts from the parish registers of Chute and Market Lavington, in the county of Wilts', *Collectanea topographica et genealogica* **8**, 1843, 190-204.

Cliffe Pypard

GODDARD, E.H. 'Marriages at Clyffe Pypard, 1576 to 1837', in PHILLIMORE, W.P.W., & SADLER, JOHN, eds. *W.P.R.M.* **10**. *P.P.R.S.* **155**. Phillimore, 1910, 69-96.

Codford St.Peter

H., J.J. 'Codford St.Peter register, Wilts', *Notes & queries for Somerset & Dorset* **13**, 1913, 124.

Parish Registers etc. continued

Codford St.Peter *continued*
'Registers of Codford St.Peter, Co.Wilts', in
CRISP, F.A., ed. *Fragmenta genealogica* N.S. 1,
1910, 1-44. 1598-1715.

Colerne
SMITH, MAXWELL H., ed. 'Marriages at Colerne,
1661 to 1812', in PHILLIMORE, W.P.W., & SADLER,
JOHN, eds. *W.P.R.M.* 4. *P.P.R.S.* 87. Phillimore,
1907, 135-52.
'Marriages at Colerne: additional', in PHILLIMORE,
W.P.W., NEVILL, EDMUND & SADLER, JOHN, eds.
W.P.R.M. 5. *P.P.R.S.* 99. Phillimore, 1907,
151-2.

Collingbourne Ducis
BARTELOT, R. GROSVENOR, & TANNER, G.F., eds.
'Marriages at Collingbourne Ducis, 1654 to
1837', in PHILLIMORE, W.P.W., & SADLER, JOHN,
eds. *W.P.R.M.* 12. *P.P.R.S.* 189. Phillimore,
1912, 133-47.
HODGSON, J.D. 'Entries in a parish register,
Collingbourne Ducis', *W.A.M.* 26(78), 1892,
320-27. Miscellaneous extracts, 17-18th c.,
including biographical notes.
W., J. 'Extracts from the registers of
Collingbourne Ducis, Collingbourne Kingston,
Burbage, and Tidcombe, Wilts', *Collectanea
topographica et genealogica* 7, 1841, 175-90.
16-18th c.

Collingbourne Kingston
See Collingbourne Ducis

Crudwell
REDFERN, J. LEMON, ed. 'Marriages at Crudwell,
1662 to 1812', in PHILLIMORE, W.P.W., & SADLER,
JOHN, eds. *W.P.R.M.* 3. *P.P.R.S.* 76. Phillimore,
1906, 73-88.

Devizes
PARRY, J.H., ed. 'Marriages at Devizes, parish of
St.John the Baptist, 1559 to 1837', in
PHILLIMORE, W.P.W., & SADLER, JOHN, eds.
W.P.R.M. 11. *P.P.R.S.* 171. Phillimore, 1911,
43-140.

Downton
'Extracts from the parish registers of Downton,
Wilts', *M.G.H.* 5th series 9, 1935-7, 20-31, 74-
6, 107-11, 139-41, 173-6 & 202-6. Marriages,
1600-1837; baptisms, 1592-1812; burials,
1602-1812. Includes monumental inscriptions.

Durnford
[PHILLIPPS, SIR T., ed.] *Parish register of
Durneford, Wilts., ab anno 1574 ad annum
1650.* [Middlehill: privately printed, 1823.]

Durrington
RUDDLE, C.S., ed. 'Marriages at Durrington, 1591
to 1812', in PHILLIMORE, W.P.W., & SADLER,
JOHN, eds. *W.P.R.M.* 2. *P.P.R.S.* 61. Phillimore,
1905, 137-52.

East Coulston
WILTSHIRE FAMILY HISTORY SOCIETY, eds. *The
bishop's transcripts and parish registers of East
Coulston: baptisms and burials, 1622-1837.*
Devizes: W.F.H.S., 1992.

East Knoyle
MILFORD, ROBERT NEWMAN, ed. 'Marriages at East
Knoyle, 1538 to 1812', in PHILLIMORE, W.P.W.,
& SADLER, JOHN, eds. *W.P.R.M.* 3. *P.P.R.S.* 76.
Phillimore, 1906, 1-36.
MILFORD, [R.N.] 'Marriages during the time of the
Commonwealth: from the registers of East or
Bishops Knoyle, Wilts', *Salisbury Field Club
transactions* 2(2), 1892-6, 116-8.

Eisey
FYNMORE, A.H.W., ed. 'Marriages at Eisey, 1575 to
1837', in PHILLIMORE, W.P.W., & SADLER, JOHN,
eds. *W.P.R.M.* 10. *P.P.R.S.* 155. Phillimore,
1910, 131-44.
WILTSHIRE FAMILY HISTORY SOCIETY, eds. *The
bishop's transcripts and parish registers of
Eisey: baptisms and burials, 1574-1837.*
Devizes: W.F.H.S., 1992.

Etchilhampton
See All Cannings

Erlestoke
WILTSHIRE FAMILY HISTORY SOCIETY, eds. *The
bishop's transcripts and parish registers of
Erlestoke: baptisms and burials, 1578-1837.*
Devizes: W.F.H.S., 1992.

Fisherton Anger
BAKER, T.H. 'Fisherton Anger register, Wilts:
Somerset and Dorset marriages', *Notes &
queries for Somerset & Dorset* 11, 1909, 277-
81.
See also Britford and Stratford Subcastle

Fugglestone St.Peter
SYMONDS, W., & BAKER, T.H., eds. 'Marriages at
Fugglestone St.Peter with Bemerton, 1608 to
1837', in PHILLIMORE, W.P.W., & SADLER, JOHN,
eds. *W.P.R.M.* 12. *P.P.R.S.* 189. Phillimore,
1912, 65-91.

Great Cheverell

WILTSHIRE FAMILY HISTORY SOCIETY. *The bishop's transcripts and parish registers of Great Cheverell: baptisms, 1622-1837.* Devizes: W.F.H.S., 1992.

WILTSHIRE FAMILY HISTORY SOCIETY. *The bishop's transcripts and parish registers of Great Cheverell: burials, 1622-1837.* Devizes: W.F.H.S., 1992.

Great Somerford

MANLEY, F.H., ed. 'Marriages at Great (or Broad) Somerford, 1707 to 1812', in PHILLIMORE, W.P.W., & SADLER, JOHN, eds. *W.P.R.M.* 6. *P.P.R.S.* 105. Phillimore, 1908, 25-33.

Grittleton

SYMONDS, W., ed. 'Marriages at Grittleton, 1573 to 1812', in PHILLIMORE, W.P.W., & SADLER, JOHN, eds. *W.P.R.M.* 1. *P.P.R.S.* 57. Phillimore, 1905, 145-56.

WILTSHIRE FAMILY HISTORY SOCIETY, eds. *The bishop's transcripts and parish registers of Grittleton: baptisms, 1576-1837.* Devizes: W.F.H.S., 1992.

Ham

See Britford

Hankerton

MANLEY, F.H., ed. 'Marriages at Hankerton, 1700 to 1837', in PHILLIMORE, W.P.W., & SADLER, JOHN, eds. *W.P.R.M.* 10. *P.P.R.S.* 155. Phillimore, 1910, 11-17.

Heytesbury

CLUTSOM, A.D., ed. 'Marriages at Heytesbury, 1654 to 1837', in PHILLIMORE, W.P.W., & SADLER, JOHN, eds. *W.P.R.M.* 10. *P.P.R.S.* 155. Phillimore, 1910, 97-124.

Huish

PARRY, J.H., ed. 'Marriages at Huish, 1684 to 1812', in PHILLIMORE, W.P.W., & SADLER, JOHN, eds. *W.P.R.M.* 7. *P.P.R.S.* 119. Phillimore, 1908, 145-7.

Hungerford

HIDDEN, NORMAN & JOYCE, eds. *Hungerford, Berks & Wilts parish register: C-M-B, 1559-1619.* N. Hidden, 1984. Hungerford is partly in Berkshire, partly in Wiltshire.

Idmiston

BAKER, THOS. H., ed. 'Marriages at Idmiston, 1577 to 1812', in PHILLIMORE, W.P.W., & SADLER, JOHN, eds. *W.P.R.M.* 8. *P.P.R.S.* 127. Phillimore, 1909, 119-43.
See also Stratford Subcastle

Imber

HURLEY, BERYL & HASSELL, MARGERY, eds. *Imber 1623-1837: the bishops' transcripts & parish registers.* [ ]: Wiltshire Family History Society, 1987.

WILTSHIRE FAMILY HISTORY SOCIETY. *The bishop's transcripts and parish registers of Imber: baptisms, marriages and burials, 1574-1837.* Devizes: W.F.H.S., 1992.

Kemble

CHOLMELEY, H.W., ed. 'Marriages at Kemble, 1679 to 1812', in PHILLIMORE, W.P.W., & SADLER, JOHN, eds. *W.P.R.M.* 6. *P.P.R.S.* 105. Phillimore, 1908, 15-23.

Kingston Deverill

BAKER, T.H., ed. 'Marriages at Kingston Deverill, 1706 to 1812', in PHILLIMORE, W.P.W., & SADLER, JOHN, eds. *W.P.R.M.* 1. *P.P.R.S.* 57. Phillimore, 1905, 93-9.

BAKER, T.H. 'Marriages of Somerset and Dorset people celebrated in other counties', *Notes & queries for Somerset & Dorset* 7, 1901, 315-6. From the registers of Kingston Deverill and Monkton Deverill, Wiltshire.

Kington

ADRIAN, A.H.W., & SYNGE, F.P., eds. 'Marriages at Kington St.Michael, 1563 to 1837', in PHILLIMORE, W.P.W., & SADLER, JOHN, eds. *W.P.R.M.* 12. *P.P.R.S.* 189. Phillimore, 1912. 29-64.

Knook

CLUTSOM, A.D., ed. 'Marriages at Knook, 1695 to 1837', in PHILLIMORE, W.P.W., & SADLER, JOHN, eds. *W.P.R.M.* 10. *P.P.R.S.* 155. Phillimore, 1910, 125-30.

Latton

FYNMORE, A.H.W., & GOTT, C.R., eds. 'Marriages at Latton, 1578 to 1837', in PHILLIMORE, W.P.W., & SADLER, JOHN, eds. *W.P.R.M.* 12. *P.P.R.S.* 189. Phillimore, 1912, 115-31.

WILTSHIRE FAMILY HISTORY SOCIETY. *The bishop's transcripts and parish registers of Latton: baptisms, 1576-1837.* Devizes: W.F.H.S., 1992.

WILTSHIRE FAMILY HISTORY SOCIETY. *The bishop's transcripts and parish registers of Latton: burials, 1628-1837.* Devizes: W.F.H.S., 1992.

Laverstock

BAKER, T.H., ed. 'Marriages at Laverstock, 1726 to 1812', in PHILLIMORE, W.P.W., & SADLER, JOHN, eds. *W.P.R.M.* 10. *P.P.R.S.* 155. Phillimore, 1910, 1-9.
See also Stratford Subcastle

Parish Registers etc. continued

Leigh Delamere
WYNN-LLOYD, W., ed. 'Marriages at Leigh Delamere, 1735 to 1812', in PHILLIMORE, W.P.W., & SADLER, JOHN, eds. *W.P.R.M.* **1.** *P.P.R.S.* **57.** Phillimore, 1905, 157-60.

Liddington
WILTSHIRE FAMILY HISTORY SOCIETY. *The bishop's transcripts and parish registers of Liddington: baptisms and burials, 1605-1837.* W.F.H.S., 1992.

Little Somerford
MANLEY, F.H. 'Marriages at Little Somerford, 1708 to 1812', in PHILLIMORE, W.P.W., & SADLER, JOHN, eds. *W.P.R.M.* **6.** *P.P.R.S.* **105.** Phillimore, 1908, 35-40.

Long Newnton
REDFERN, J. LEMON, ed. 'Marriages at Long Newnton, 1653 to 1812', in PHILLIMORE, W.P.W., & SADLER, JOHN, eds. *W.P.R.M.* **3.** *P.P.R.S.* **76.** Phillimore, 1906, 101-22.

Luckington
SYMONDS, W., ed. 'Marriages at Luckington, 1573 to 1837', in PHILLIMORE, W.P.W., & SADLER, JOHN, eds. *W.P.R.M.* **11.** *P.P.R.S.* **171.** Phillimore, 1911, 141-52.

Lydiard Millicent
HARRISON, D. PERCY, ed. 'Marriages at Lydiard Millicent, 1580 to 1837', in PHILLIMORE, W.P.W., & SADLER, JOHN, eds. *W.P.R.M.* **8.** *P.P.R.S.* **127.** Phillimore, 1909, 23-36.

Malmesbury
THOMAS, B.C. 'Extracts from the parish register of Malmesbury, Co.Wilts', *Collectanea topographica et genealogica* 6, 1840, 237-44.

Manningford Abbots
WILTSHIRE FAMILY HISTORY SOCIETY. *The bishop's transcripts and parish registers of Manningford Abbots: baptisms, 1539-1837.* Devizes: W.F.H.S., 1992.
WILTSHIRE FAMILY HISTORY SOCIETY. *The bishop's transcripts and parish registers of Manningford Abbots and Manningford Bruce: burials.* Devizes: W.F.H.S., 1992.

Manningford Bruce
WILTSHIRE FAMILY HISTORY SOCIETY. *The bishop's transcripts and parish registers of Manningford Bruce: baptisms, 1605-1837.* Devizes: W.F.H.S., 1992.
See also Manningford Abbots.

Marden
PARRY, J.H., ed. 'Marriages at Marden, 1693 to 1812', in PHILLIMORE, W.P.W., & SADLER, JOHN, eds. *W.P.R.M.* **6.** *P.P.R.S.* **105.** Phillimore, 1908, 117-21.
WILTSHIRE FAMILY HISTORY SOCIETY, eds. *The bishop's transcripts and parish registers of Marden: baptisms, 1622-1837.* Devizes: W.F.H.S., 1992.

Market Lavington
STURTON, J.A., & SYMONDS, W., eds. 'Marriages at Market Lavington alias Lavington Forum, 1673 to 1812', in PHILLIMORE, W.P.W., & SADLER, JOHN, eds. *W.P.R.M.* **8.** *P.P.R.S.* **127.** Phillimore, 1909, 63-91.
WILTSHIRE FAMILY HISTORY SOCIETY, eds. *The bishop's transcripts and parish registers of Market Lavington: baptisms, 1622-1837.* 2 vols. Devizes: W.F.H.S., 1992. Vol.1. 1622-1787. Vol.2. 1787-1837.
See also Chute

Marlborough
GWILLIM, E.LL., ed. 'Marriages at Marlborough (parish of St.Mary the Virgin), 1602-1812', in PHILLIMORE, W.P.W., & SADLER, JOHN, eds. *W.P.R.M.* **2.** *P.P.R.S.* **61.** Phillimore, 1905, 65-125.
GWILLIM, E.LL., ed. 'Marriages at Marlborough (parish of St.Peter and St.Paul the Apostles), 1611 to 1812', in PHILLIMORE, W.P.W., & SADLER, JOHN, eds. *W.P.R.M.* **2.** *P.P.R.S.* **61.** Phillimore, 1905, 1-64.
W., J. 'Extracts from the registers of the parishes of St.Peter and St.Paul the apostles, and St.Mary the Virgin, Marlborough, with the most important of unpublished epitaphs', *Collectanea topographica et genealogica* 5, 1838, 260-74.

Martin
See Netheravon

Melksham
'Extracts from the registers of Melksham', *Genealogist* 3, 1879, 399. 18th c.

Mere
BAKER, T.H., ed. 'Marriages at Mere, 1561 to 1812', in PHILLIMORE, W.P.W., & SADLER, JOHN, eds. *W.P.R.M.* **1.** *P.P.R.S.* **57.** Phillimore, 1905, 1-87.
BAKER, THOS. H. 'Wolstan', *Notes & queries for Somerset & Dorset* 6, 1899, 224. Baptisms with an unusual first name, i.e. Wolstan, at Mere.

Parish Registers etc. continued

Mildenhall

See Preshute

Milston

RUDDLE, C.S., ed. 'Marriages at Milston, 1540 to 1812', in PHILLIMORE, W.P.W., & SADLER, JOHN, eds. *W.P.R.M.* **3**. *P.P.R.S.* **76**. Phillimore, 1906, 123-8.

Milton Lilborne

W., J. 'Extracts from the parish registers of Milton Lislebon, near Pewsey, Co.Wilts', *Topographer & genealogist* **3**, 1858, 347-52.

Minety

MANLEY, F.H., ed. 'Marriages at Minety, 1663 to 1812', in PHILLIMORE, W.P.W., & SADLER, JOHN, eds. *W.P.R.M.* **8**. *P.P.R.S.* **127**. Phillimore, 1909, 37-61.

Monkton Deverill

BAKER, T.H., ed. 'Marriages at Monkton Deverill, 1749 to 1812', in PHILLIMORE, W.P.W., & SADLER, JOHN, eds. *W.P.R.M.* **1**. *P.P.R.S.* **57**. Phillimore, 1905, 89-91.

See also Kingston Deverill

Netheravon

'Somerset and Dorset marriages', *Notes & queries for Somerset & Dorset* **14**, 1915, 135. From the parish registers of Netheravon, Martin and Wylye.

Newton Tony

RUDDLE, C.S., ed. 'Marriages at Newton Tony, 1591 to 1812', in PHILLIMORE, W.P.W., & SADLER, JOHN, eds. *W.P.R.M.* **3**. *P.P.R.S.* **76**. Phillimore, 1906, 133-42.

North Bradley

WILTSHIRE FAMILY HISTORY SOCIETY, eds. *The bishop's transcripts and parish registers of North Bradley: baptisms, 1603-1837*. 2 vols. Devizes: W.F.H.S., 1992. Vol.1. 1603-1766. Vol.2. 1767-1837.

North Wraxall

HARRISON, FRANCIS. *Annals of the parish of North Wraxhall, Wilts*. Bath: Charles Higgins, 1906. Primarily an alphabetical list of births, marriages and deaths from the parish register; also includes other miscellaneous information.

Norton

WARNEFORD, H.L., ed. 'Marriages at Norton', in PHILLIMORE, W.P.W., & SADLER, JOHN, eds. *W.P.R.M.* **5**. *P.P.R.S.* **99**. Phillimore, 1907, 147-50.

Ogbourne St.Andrew

See Preshute

Ogbourne St.George

See Preshute

Patney

PARRY, J.H., ed. 'Marriages at Patney, 1594 to 1812', in PHILLIMORE, W.P.W., & SADLER, JOHN, eds. *W.P.R.M.* **6**. *P.P.R.S.* **105**. Phillimore, 1908, 93-9.

Porton

'Marriages at Porton, 1754 to 1812', in PHILLIMORE, W.P.W., & SADLER, JOHN, eds. *W.P.R.M.* **3**. *P.P.R.S.* **127**. Phillimore, 1909, 143-6.

Preshute

GWILLIM, E. LL., ed. 'Marriages at Preshute, 1606 to 1812', in PHILLIMORE, W.P.W., & SADLER, JOHN, eds. *W.P.R.M.* **4**. *P.P.R.S.* **87**. Phillimore, 1907, 1-65.

GWILLIM, E. LL., ed. 'Notes from the register books of the parish of Preshute during the 17th century', *W.A.M.* **30**(90), 1898, 100-16. Includes a few extracts, but mainly concerned with matters other than births, marriages and deaths.

W., J. 'Extracts from the registers of Preshute, Mildenhall, Ogbourne St.Andrew, and Ogbourne St.George, Wilts., with some of the most important and unpublished epitaphs', *Collectanea topographica et genealogica* **5**, 1838, 346-59.

Purton

STORY-MASKELYNE, A.ST.J., ed. 'Marriages at Purton, 1558 to 1812', in PHILLIMORE, W.P.W., & SADLER, JOHN, eds. *W.P.R.M.* **7**. *P.P.R.S.* **119**. Phillimore, 1908, 99-140.

Rollstone

BAKER, T.H., ed. 'Marriages at Rollestone, 1654 to 1812', in PHILLIMORE, W.P.W., & SADLER, JOHN, eds. *W.P.R.M.* **6**. *P.P.R.S.* **105**. Phillimore, 1908, 149-52.

Salisbury

W., H.J. 'Unknown parish register', *W.N.Q.* **1**, 1893-5, 172-3. Extracts from register, June-July 1737, for an unknown parish—possibly in Salisbury.

Salisbury Cathedral

MALDEN, A.R. 'A Salisbury fifteenth century death register', 1467-75', *Ancestor* **9**, 1904, 28-35. Deaths connected with the Cathedral.

Parish Registers etc. continued

Salisbury Cathedral continued
SYMONDS, W., ed. 'Marriages at Salisbury (the Cathedral), 1564 to 1812', in PHILLIMORE, W.P.W., & SADLER, JOHN, eds. *W.P.R.M.* 7. *P.P.R.S.* 119. Phillimore, 1908, 1-93.

Salisbury. St.Edmund
THURLOW, A.R. & PARSONS, JAMES, eds. 'Marriages at Salisbury (Parish of St.Edmund), 1559 to 1837', in SADLER, JOHN, ed. *W.P.R.M.* 13, 1913, 1-146, and 14, 1914, 1-113. (*P.P.R.S.* 144 & 212.)

Salisbury. St.Martin
BAKER, THOMAS H., ed. 'Marriages at Salisbury (Parish of St.Martin), 1559 to 1812', in PHILLIMORE, W.P.W., BAKER, THOMAS H., & SADLER, JOHN, ᐁds. *W.P.R.M.* 9. *P.P.R.S.* 150. Phillimore, 1910, 1-155.
BAKER, T. 'Somerset and Dorset marriages', *Notes & queries for Somerset & Dorset* 10, 1907, 121-2; 12, 1911, 131-4. At St.Martins, Salisbury. 'Strays from Salisbury', *Greenwood tree* 6(2), 1981, 30. Somerset and Dorset entries from the parish registers of St.Martins, Salisbury, 1693-1799.

Salisbury. St.Thomas
FORSTER-BROWN, S., ed. 'Marriages at Salisbury (parish of St.Thomas), 1570 to 1812', in PHILLIMORE, W.P.W., NEVILL, EDMUND, & SADLER, JOHN, eds. *W.P.R.M.* 5. *P.P.R.S.* 99. Phillimore, 1907, 1-134.

Seend
S[CHOMBERG], A. 'Extracts of Seend, Co.Wilts', *Genealogist* 3, 1879, 387-98.

Semington
WILTSHIRE FAMILY HISTORY SOCIETY, eds. *The bishop's transcripts and parish registers of Semington: baptisms, 1586-1837.* Devizes: W.F.H.S., 1992.

Sherrington
HAMMOND, J.J., ed. 'Marriages at Sherrington, 1677 to 1837', in PHILLIMORE, W.P.W., & SADLER, JOHN, eds. *W.P.R.M.* 12. *P.P.R.S.* 189. Phillimore, 1912, 109-13.

Sherston Magna
SYMONDS, W., ed. 'Marriages at Sherston Magna, 1653 to 1812', in PHILLIMORE, W.P.W., & SADLER, JOHN, eds. *W.P.R.M.* 1. *P.P.R.S.* 57. Phillimore, 1905, 101-29.

Slaughterford
KETCHLEY, H.E. 'Quaker marriages at Slaughterford', *W.A.M.* 49(176), 1942, 562-4. 17-18th c.

Sopworth
SYMONDS, W., ed. 'Marriages at Sopworth, 1698 to 1812', in PHILLIMORE, W.P.W., & SADLER, JOHN, eds. *W.P.R.M.* 1. *P.P.R.S.* 57. Phillimore, 1905, 141-4.

Southbroom
PARRY, J.H., ed. 'Marriages at Southbroom, 1572 to 1837', in PHILLIMORE, W.P.W., & SADLER, JOHN, eds. *W.P.R.M.* 6. *P.P.R.S.* 105. Phillimore, 1908, 41-92.

Stert
HILL, J. HAMLYN, ed. 'Marriages at Stert, 1579 to 1812', in PHILLIMORE, W.P.W., & SADLER, JOHN, eds. *W.P.R.M.* 4. *P.P.R.S.* 87. Phillimore, 1907, 127-34.
WILTSHIRE FAMILY HISTORY SOCIETY, eds. *The bishop's transcripts and parish registers of Stert: baptisms, 1586-1837.* Devizes: W.F.H.S., 1992.

Stockton
JOHNSTONE, C.J., ed. 'Marriages at Stockton, 1590 to 1812', in PHILLIMORE, W.P.W., & SADLER, JOHN, eds. *W.P.R.M.* 3. *P.P.R.S.* 76. Phillimore, 1906, 89-100.

Stourton
ELLIS, JOHN HENRY, ed. *The registers of Stourton, County Wilts, from 1570 to 1800.* Register Section 12. Harleian Society, 1887.
BELLENGER, DOMINIC ARDAN. 'The Bonham mission', *ECA Journal* 2(1) 1986 12-14. Notes on the Catholic registers of Stourton.

Stratford Subcastle
BAKER, THOS. H., ed. 'Marriages at Stratford-Sub-Castle, 1654 to 1837', in SADLER, JOHN, ed. *W.P.R.M.* 14. *P.P.R.S.* 212. Phillimore, 1914, 115-31.
BAKER, T.H. 'Somerset and Dorset marriages', *Notes & queries for Somerset & Dorset* 12, 1911, 165-6. From Stratford Subcastle, Fisherton Anger, West Barnham, Idmiston and Laverstock.

Tidcombe
See Collingbourne Ducis

Parish Registers etc. continued

Tilshead
WILTSHIRE FAMILY HISTORY SOCIETY, eds. *The bishop's transcripts and parish registers of Tilshead: baptisms, 1603-1837.* Devizes: W.F.H.S., 1992.

Tytherton
'Strays: registers of Tytherton Moravian church, Wiltshire', *Journal of the Bristol & Avon Family History Society* **49**, 1987, 21-24. Entries relating to Bristol and Gloucestershire strays.

Urchfont
COLE, JEAN A. 'Some interesting burial entries from the Urchfont parish registers', *W.F.H.S.* **15**, 1984, 15. 1695-1727.

HILL, J. HAMLYN, ed. 'Marriages at Urchfont, alias Erchfont', in PHILLIMORE, W.P.W., & SADLER, JOHN, eds. *W.P.R.M.* **4**. *P.P.R.S.* **87**. Phillimore, 1907, 67-125.

West Barnham
See Stratford Subcastle

Westbury Union
BLAKE, PAUL A. 'Deaths in the Westbury and Whorwellsdown poor law union workhouse, 1836-1840', *W.F.H.S.* **27**, 1987, 16-18.

West Knoyle
GRIFFITH, G.W. 'Marriages at West Knoyle, 1719 to 1837', in PHILLIMORE, W.P.W., & SADLER, JOHN, eds. *W.P.R.M.* **10**. *P.P.R.S.* **155**. Phillimore, 1910, 145-9.

West Lavington
ROE, HERBERT F. 'Extracts from the parish register of West or Bishop's Lavington, Co.Wilts', *Genealogist* N.S. **4**, 1887, 68-71.

West Wellow
EMPSON, CHARLES W. *Index to the registers of baptisms, marriages & burials of the parish of Wellow, in the counties of Southampton and Wiltshire with an appendix containing an index to briefs collected at Wellow, lists of vicars and churchwardens, and other matters.* Eyre & Spottiswoode, 1889. East Wellow, Hampshire; West Wellow, Wiltshire.

Whiteparish
HILL, ARTHUR, ed. 'Marriages at Whiteparish, 1560 to 1837', in PHILLIMORE, W.P.W., & SADLER, JOHN, eds. *W.P.R.M.* **11**. *P.P.R.S.* **171**. Phillimore, 1911, 1-42.

Whorwellsdown Union
See Westbury Union

Winterslow
SYMONDS, W., ed. 'Marriages at Winterslow, 1598 to 1812', in PHILLIMORE, W.P.W., & SADLER, JOHN, eds. *W.P.R.M.* **6**. *P.P.R.S.* **105**. Phillimore, 1908, 129-48.

Woodborough
STURTON, J.A., ed. 'Marriages at Woodborough, 1567 to 1837', in PHILLIMORE, W.P.W., & SADLER, JOHN, eds. *W.P.R.M.* **8**. *P.P.R.S.* **127**. Phillimore, 1909, 105-118.

Wylye
BAKER, T.H., & HAMMOND, J.J. *The registers of the parish of Wylye in the County of Wilts.* Devizes: G.R. Hadow, 1913.
See also Britford and Netheravon

Yatesbury
WILTSHIRE FAMILY HISTORY SOCIETY, eds. *The bishop's transcripts and parish registers of Yatesbury: baptisms, 1606-1837.* Devizes: W.F.H.S., 1992.

Yatton Keynell
WYLD, C.N., & SYMONDS, W., eds. 'Marriages at Yatton Keynell, 1653 to 1812', in PHILLIMORE, W.P.W., & SADLER, JOHN, eds. *W.P.R.M.* **2**. *P.P.R.S.* **61**. Phillimore, 1905, 127-36.

9. MONUMENTAL INSCRIPTIONS

A. GENERAL

Monumental inscriptions are an important source of genealogical information. Many have been copied; one collection of transcripts is listed in:

GODDARD, E.H. 'The collection of ms. copies of the monumental inscriptions in the churches and churchyards of Wiltshire in the Society's library', *W.A.M.* **44**(147), 1927, 10-13.

A major survey, now very rare, is:

PHILLIPPS, SIR T. *Monumental inscriptions in the county of Wilton*. Middle Hill: Typis Medio-Montanis, 1822.

Brief descriptions of monuments in many Wiltshire churches are provided by:

ROBINSON, W.J. *West country churches*. 4 vols. Bristol: Bristol Times & Mirror, 1914-16. This also covers Gloucestershire and East Somerset.

Two general guides to Wiltshire brasses are available:

LEETE-HODGE, LORNIE. *A guide to Wiltshire brasses*. Tisbury: Compton Press, 1977.

KITE, EDWARD. *The monumental brasses of Wiltshire: a series of examples of these memorials, ranging from the thirteenth to the seventeenth centuries, accompanied with notices descriptive of ancient costumes, and generally illustrative of the history of the county during this period*. J.H. & J. Parker, 1860. Reprinted Bath: Kingsmead Bookshop, 1969. Includes some pedigrees.

See also:

SADLER, A.G. *The indents of lost monumental brasses in Wiltshire*. Worthing: the author, 1975. Appendix published 1980.

For heraldry, see:

BATTERSBY, R. ST.JOHN B. 'Heraldry of the churches of Wiltshire', *W.A.M.* **44**(150), 1929, 360-71; **44**(151), 1929, 418-28; **45**(153), 1930, 147-55.

SCHOMBERG, A. 'Church heraldry of North Wiltshire', *W.A.M.* **22**(66), 1885, 335-9; **23**, 1887, 40-50, 200-210 & 299-313; **24**, 1889, 44-57 & 287-307; **25**, 1891, 100-111.

Wiltshire hatchments are given in:

SUMMERS, PETER. *Hatchments in Britain, 4: Bedfordshire, Berkshire, Buckinghamshire, Oxfordshire and Wiltshire*. Chichester: Phillimore, 1983.

For burials of the bishops of Salisbury, see:

MALDEN, A.R. 'The burial places of the Bishops of Salisbury', *W.A.M.* **37**(117), 1912, 339-52.

B. BY PLACE

Alton Berners

SCHOMBERG, ARTHUR. 'Monumental inscriptions of Alton Berners, Co.Wilts', *M.G.H.* 2nd series **4**, 1892, 186-7.

Alton Priors

SCHOMBERG, ARTHUR. 'Monumental inscriptions of Alton Priors, Co.Wilts', *M.G.H.* 2nd series **4**, 1892, 186-7.

Atworth

SCHOMBERG, ARTHUR. 'The monumental inscriptions of Atworth or Atford, Co.Wilts', *M.G.H.* 2nd series **4**, 1892, 130-32.

Beechingstoke

SCHOMBERG, ARTHUR. 'Monumental inscriptions of Beechingstoke, Co.Wilts', *M.G.H.* 3rd series **1**, 1896, 17-18.

Biddestone

SCHOMBERG, ARTHUR. 'Monumental inscriptions of Biddestone and Slaughterford churches, Co.Wilts', *M.G.H.* 2nd series **5**, 1894, 65-7.

Box

SCHOMBERG, ARTHUR. 'The monumental inscriptions of Box church, Co.Wilts', *Genealogist* N.S. **10**, 1894, 178-83.

Bradford on Avon

SCHOMBERG, ARTHUR. 'Monumental inscriptions of Holy Trinity, Bradford-on-Avon, Co.Wilts', *M.G.H.* 2nd series **3**, 1890, 89-91, 100-102, 118-21, 146-50 & 173-4.

Broughton Gifford

SCHOMBERG, ARTHUR. 'The monumental inscriptions of Broughton Gifford, Co.Wilts', *M.G.H.* 2nd series **4**, 1892, 127-8.

Calne

SCHOMBERG, ARTHUR. 'The monumental inscriptions of Calne church, Co.Wilts', *Genealogist* N.S. **14**, 1898, 37-44 & 90-94. See also 212.

Chalfield Magna

SCHOMBERG, ARTHUR. 'Monumental inscriptions of Great Chaldfield, Co.Wilts', *M.G.H.* 3rd series **1**, 1896, 125-6.

Chippenham

SCHOMBERG, ARTHUR. 'The monumental inscriptions of Chippenham parish church, Co.Wilts', *Genealogist* **6**, 1890, 199-206, and **7**, 1891, 47-53.

Monumental Inscriptions continued

Chippenham District

AWDRY, EDWARD C. 'A paper on monumental brasses in some of the churches near Chippenham', *W.A.M.* **12**(25), 1870, 233-44.

Cholderton

BARROW, EDWIN P. *Parish notes.* Salisbury: Brown & Co., 1889. Concerns Cholderton; includes monumental inscriptions, and a list of documents in the parish chest, etc.

Corsham

BRAKSPEAR, HAROLD. *The church of St.Bartholomew at Corsham in Wiltshire.* Devizes: George Simpson & Co., 1924. Includes monumental inscriptions, list of clergy, etc.

SCHOMBERG, A. 'Monumental inscriptions in Corsham church', *W.N.Q.* **4**, 1902-4, 510-15. Discussion.

SCHOMBERG, ARTHUR. 'The monumental inscriptions of Corsham church, Co.Wilts', *M.G.H.* 2nd series **4**, 1892, 305-7, 332-4, 348-9 & 358-61; 4th series **1**, 1906, 190-91.

Cricklade

R-B., T.T. 'Monumental inscriptions in St.Mary's churchyard, Cricklade, 1976', *Cricklade Historical Society bulletin* **2**(1), 1976, 6-7. List of 67 inscriptions, giving ages and dates. 'The names on the war memorial', *Cricklade Historical Society bulletin* **2**(10), 1989, 7-11.

Ditteridge

SCHOMBERG, ARTHUR. 'Monumental inscriptions of Ditcheridge, Co.Wilts', *M.G.H.* 3rd series **1**, 1896, 58-9.

East Coulston

WILTON, EDWARD. 'Coffin plates recently discovered at East Coulston, Wilts', *W.A.M.* **3**(7), 1855, 97-106. Includes pedigrees of Lambe and Godolphin. 16-18th c.

Fonthill Abbey

SIMPSON, JUSTIN. 'An account of the armorial decorations formerly in the windows of Fonthill Abbey, Wilts', *Reliquary* **7**, 1866-7, 109-12 & 167-72.

Holt

SCHOMBERG, A. 'The monumental inscriptions of Holt, Co.Wilts', *M.G.H.* 2nd series **2**, 1888, 130-31 & 155-7.

Lacock

SCHOMBERG, ARTHUR. 'Monumental inscriptions of Lacock church, Co.Wilts', *Genealogist* **7**, 1883, 241-2.

BROCKLEBANK, G.R. *The heraldry of the church of St.Cyriac, in Lacock.* Melksham: Uffington Press, 1968.

Langley Burrell

See Tytherton Lucas

Limpley Stoke

SCHOMBERG, A. 'The monumental inscriptions of Limpley Stoke, Co.Wilts', *M.G.H.* 2nd series **2**, 1888, 91-3.

Lydiard Tregoze

HUSSEY, CHRISTOPHER. 'Monuments at Lydiard Tregoz', *Country life* **103**, 1948, 726-9 & 778-81.

Maddington

S[CHOMBERG], A. 'Monumental inscriptions at Maddington, Co.Wilts', *M.G.H.* N.S. **3**, 1880, 329-30.

Manningford Bruce

S[CHOMBERG], A. 'The monumental inscriptions at Manningford Bruce, Co.Wilts', *M.G.H.* N.S. **4**, 1884, 201.

Marden

SCHOMBERG, ARTHUR. 'Monumental inscriptions of Marden, Co.Wilts', *M.G.H.* 3rd series **1**, 1896, 143-4.

North Newnton

SCHOMBERG, ARTHUR. 'Monumental inscriptions of North Newnton, Co.Wilts', *M.G.H.* 2nd series **3**, 1890, 390-91.

Pewsey

SCHOMBERG, ARTHUR. 'Monumental inscriptions of Pewsey, Co.Wilts', *M.G.H.* 2nd series **1**, 1886, 273-6.

Ramsbury

WEBB, EDWARD DORAN. *The history of the Hundred of Ramsbury in the county of Wiltshire: v.1. The parish of Ramsbury.* Salisbury: Bennett Bros., 1890. Includes monumental inscriptions, lists of clergy, etc. The only volume published.

Rushall

SCHOMBERG, ARTHUR. 'The monumental inscriptions of Rushall, Co.Wilts', *M.G.H.* 2nd series **3**, 1890, 43-4.

Monumental Inscriptions continued

Salisbury

REEVES, JOHN A. *An abstract of monumental inscriptions in Salisbury churches*. Salisbury: Salisbury Museum, 1975.

Salisbury Cathedral

There are many published works on Salisbury Cathedral; those which give monumental inscriptions include:

BAKER, THOMAS HENRY. 'Monumental inscriptions and heraldry in Salisbury Cathedral: Baker manuscripts collection', *Notes & queries* 12th series **1**, 1916, 425-6. Index to a ms. collection of inscriptions.

BAKER, T.H. 'Somerset and Dorset inscriptions in Salisbury Cathedral', *Notes & queries for Somerset & Dorset* **10**, 1907, 127-30, 179-80 & 229-30.

COWAN, MICHAEL. 'Military memorials in the Cathedral', *Spire: annual report of the Friends of Salisbury Cathedral* **57**, 1987, 17-19.

DODSWORTH, WILLIAM. *An historical account of the episcopal see and Cathedral church of Sarum, or Salisbury, comprising biographical notices of the bishops, the history of the establishment from the earliest period, and a description of the monuments*. Salisbury: the author, 1814.

DORLING, E.E. 'Notes on some armorial glass in Salisbury Cathedral', *Ancestor* **4**, 1903, 120-26.

DORLING, E.E. 'Notes on the heraldry of Salisbury Cathedral', *W.A.M.* **29**(87), 113-22. Includes pedigree of Seymour and Grey, medieval.

HARRIS, JAMES. *Copies of the epitaphs in Salisbury Cathedral, cloisters and cemetery, accompanied by translations, notes historical and biographical, with a general survey of the other churches in Salisbury, and a concise history of the family of Montacute, Earls of Salisbury*. Salisbury: Brodie & Dowding, 1825.

PLANCHE, J.R. 'On the sepulchral effigies in Salisbury Cathedral', *Journal of the British Archaeological Association* **15**, 1859, 115-30.

SPRING, ROY. *Salisbury Cathedral*. New Bell's Cathedral guides. Unwin Hyman, 1987. Includes a chapter on the monuments, with lists of bishops and deans.

SYMONDS, RICHARD. *Diary of the marches of the royal army during the great civil war*. ed. Charles Edward Long. Camden Society original series **74**, 1859. For inscriptions in Salisbury Cathedral in the 17th c., see 129-40.

A description of that adminirable structure, the Cathedral Church of Salisbury, with the chapels, monuments, gravestones, and their inscriptions, to which is prefixed an account of Old Sarum. R. Baldwin, 1774.

The history and antiquities of the Cathedral Church of Salisbury and the Abbey Church of Bath. W. Mears & J. Hooke, 1723. Includes monumental inscriptions.

Salisbury. St.Thomas

BELLASIS, EDWARD. *Monumental inscriptions within the church of St.Thomas, Salisbury*. ed. F.E. Trotman. Salisbury: Bennett Bros., 1907.

Seend

'Monumental inscriptions at Seend, Co.Wilts', *Genealogist* **3**, 1879, 282-3 & 315-22; **4**, 1880, 123-5; N.S. **3**, 1886, 245-6. See also addenda, N.S. **28**, 1912, 175-9.

'Seend monumental inscriptions', *Genealogist* N.S. **34**, 1918, 74-9 & 120-25; **35**, 1919, 17-25 & 216-25; **36**, 1920, 126-34. Includes many wills, with a pedigree of Somner, 17-18th c.

Semington

SCHOMBERG, ARTHUR. 'The monumental inscriptions of Semington church, Co.Wilts', *Genealogist* N.S. **6**, 1890, 116-9. Includes extracts from the parish register.

Shrewton

'The monumental inscriptions at Shrewton, Co.Wilts', *M.G.H.* N.S. **3**, 1880, 279-80.

Slaughterford

See Biddestone

South Wraxall

SCHOMBERG, ARTHUR. 'The monumental inscriptions of South Wraxall, Co.Wilts', *M.G.H.* 2nd series **2**, 1888, 360-2.

Stanton St.Bernard

SCHOMBERG, ARTHUR. 'The monumental inscriptions of Stanton St.Bernard, Co.Wilts', *Genealogist* N.S. **9**, 1893, 34-6.

Tytherton Lucas

'The monumental inscriptions (other than Stokes) of Tytherton Lucas, Co.Wilts', *M.G.H.* N.S. **4**, 1884, 26-8. Also includes inscriptions from Langley Burrell.

'Monuments in Tytherton Lucas church, Co.Wilts', *M.G.H.* N.S. **3**, 1880, 330.

Upavon

SCHOMBERG, ARTHUR. 'The monumental inscriptions of Upavon, Co.Wilts', *M.G.H.* 2nd series **2**, 1888, 379-81.

Westwood
WERE, F. 'Shield of arms in Westwood church',
W.N.Q. **4**, 1902-4, 272-3.

Whadddon
SCHOMBERG, ARTHUR. 'The monumental
inscriptions of Whaddon, Co.Wilts', *M.G.H.*
2nd series **2**, 1888, 325-7.

Winsley
'Monumental inscriptions of Winsley church,
Co.Wilts', *M.G.H.* 2nd series **5**, 1894, 166-7.

Winterbourne Bassett
HOLLAENDER, ALBERT. 'A note on the recumbent
effigies at St.Katharine and St.Peter's,
Winterbourne Bassett', *W.A.M.* **49**(175), 1941,
386-90.

Woodborough
SCHOMBERG, ARTHUR. 'Monumental inscriptions
of Woodborough, Co.Wilts', *M.G.H.* 2nd series
3, 1890, 395-6.

C. *BY FAMILY*
Aubrey
'Monumental brass to the grandfather of John
Aubrey, the Wiltshire antiquary', *W.N.Q.* **5**,
1905-7, 323-4. Includes pedigree, 17th c.

Barnston
DORLING, E.E. 'A hatchment in Salisbury
Cathedral', *Salisbury Field Club transactions* **2**,
1892-6, 73-4. Barnston family.

Baynard
KITE, EDWARD. 'Baynard monuments in Lacock
church', *W.A.M.* **4**(1), 1858, 1-8. Includes
pedigree, 15-17th c.

Baynton
'A Baynton monument in the Mayor's Chapel,
Bristol', *W.A.M.* **3**, 1899-1901, 241. See also
336 & 560. 1667. Wiltshire family.

Bennet
NORRIS, MALCOLM. 'The Bennett brasses at Norton
Bavant and Westbury, Wiltshire', *Monumental
Brass Society transactions* **11**, 1971, 162-70.

Bradford
PARSONS, W.F. 'Bradford inscriptions at Broad
Hinton', *W.N.Q.* **1**, 1893-5, 284. See also 329.
Bradford family.

Bridport
SHORTT, H. DE S. 'The tomb of Bishop Giles de
Bridport', *Friends of Salisbury Cathedral
annual report* **30**, 1960, 9-12.

Brodrick
See Daubeney

Bulstrode
KITE, EDWARD. 'Bulstrode tomb formerly in
Erlestoke church', *W.N.Q.* **7**, 1911-13, 251-7.

Chaz
TALBOT, C.H. 'The gravestone of Albert de Chaz',
W.A.M. **28**(83), 1895, 146-9. 12th c.

Cobb
WERE, F. 'Cobb heraldry in Corsham church',
M.G.H. 4th series **1**, 1906, 275.

Daubeney
'Two Wiltshire monuments', *W.N.Q.* **5**, 1905-7,
481-6. To Philip Daubeney, 1236, and Sir
Thomas Brodrick, 1641; includes Brodrick's
will, 1638.

Fitzalan
TALBOT, C.H. 'Arms of Fitzalan, Earl of Arundel,
at Keevil', *W.N.Q.* **2**, 1896-8, 33-5. At Talboys
House, Keevil.

Giffard
BARON, J. 'Early heraldry in Boyton church, Wilts:
recovery of a missing link', *W.A.M.* **20**(59),
1882, 145-54. Giffard and Plantagenet arms.

Goddard
'Goddard brass in Aldbourn church', *W.A.M.*
11(33), 1869, 339-40. 15th c.

Gorges
ESDAILE, K.A. 'The Gorges monument in Salisbury
Cathedral', *W.A.M.* **50**(177), 1942, 53-62. 1610.
FLETCHER, J.M.J. 'The Gorges monument in
Salisbury Cathedral', *W.A.M.* **46**(157), 1932,
16-34. 16-17th c.
FLETCHER, J.M.J. *The Gorges monument in
Salisbury Cathedral: a lecture.* Devizes: G.
Simpson, 1932. Reprinted from the *Wiltshire
gazette.* 16-17th c.

Grey
EGERTON, SIR PHILIP GREY. 'On a monumental
brass in Christ Church Cathedral, Dublin',
Archaeological journal **36**, 1879, 213-8. Grey
family of Wilton. 16-17th c.
KING, THOMAS WILLIAM. 'Observations on the
monumental inscription to Richard Grey, Lord
Grey de Wilton, in the chapel of Eton College,
Bucks', *Archaeologia* **32**, 1847, 58-9. 1521.
Includes pedigree, 14-16th c.

Monumental Inscriptions continued

Grove

'Inventory of Jane Grove's goods and chattels',
Notes & queries for Somerset & Dorset 22,
1938, 175-7. Salisbury; 1665.

Hertford

FLETCHER, J.M.J. *The Hertford monument in
Salisbury Cathedral*. Devizes: George Simpson,
1927. 17th c.

ROBERTSON, D.H. 'The Hertford monument',
Friends of Salisbury Cathedral annual report
16, 1946, 9-10.

Hillman

BAKER, T. 'Hillman family', *W.N.Q.* 7, 1911-13,
528. Monumental inscriptions at West Knoyle.

Hungerford

FLETCHER, J.M.J. 'The monument of Robert Lord
Hungerford', *W.A.M.* 47(165), 1936, 457-65.
15th c.

FLETCHER, J.M.J. 'The tomb of Lord Walter
Hungerford, K.G., in Salisbury Cathedral',
W.A.M. 47(165), 1936, 447-56. 15th c., with
notes on medieval family, and list of chaplains
of his chantry, 15-16th c.

Hyde

DORLING, E.E. 'Notes on the arms of Hyde',
Salisbury Field Club transactions 2, 1892-6,
119-22.

Long

FYNMORE, A.H.W. 'Long family of Jamaica', *Notes
& queries* 165, 1933, 339-40. Monumental
inscriptions relating to a branch of the Wiltshire
Long family resident in Jamaica and Surrey,
18th c.

LUCKETT, LARRY. 'An eighteenth century
tombstone from Bratton', *W.A.M.* 83, 1990,
213-5. Jemima Long, nee Nevill, 1769.

Longespee

CARRINGTON, F.A. 'On monumental figures
discovered at Wanborough, Wilts', *Journal of
the British Archaeological Association* 7, 1852,
52-6. Probably of the Longespee family;
medieval.

DRURY, G.D. 'The Longespee family', *Friends of
Salisbury Cathedral annual report* 24, 1954,
9-16. Monumental inscriptions.

Metford

DORLING, E.E. 'Fifteenth century heraldry',
Ancestor 12, 1904, 146-8. Tomb of Richard
Metford, Bishop of Salisbury, 1407.

Montagu

DORLING, E.E. 'Notes on the Montagu monument
in Salisbury Cathedral', *Ancestor* 6, 1903, 46-8.
To Sir John Montagu, 1396.

Nevill

DORLING, E.E. 'Notes on two Nevill shields at
Salisbury', *Ancestor* 8, 1904, 202-4.
See also Long

Phipps

ROSE, JANET R. 'The Phipps memorial tablets at
Westbury, Wiltshire', *Journal of the Bristol &
Avon Family History Society* 22, 1980, 20-22.

Plantagenet

See Giffard

Powlett

ROGERS, W.H.H. 'The Powlett brass, Minety
church, Wilts', *Notes & queries for Somerset &
Dorset* 6, 1899, 193-6.

Sadler

'Wroughton: Sadler monumental inscriptions',
W.N.Q. 5, 1905-7, 517-20.

Seymour

BRAILSFORD, W. 'The monuments of the Seymours
in Great Bedwyn church, Wilts',
Archaeological journal 39, 1882, 407-9.

Steward

S., N.H. 'Monument of Charles Steward, esq., at
Bradford, Wiltshire', *Herald & genealogist* 2,
1865, 64-7. 1701.

Stone

KITE, EDWARD. 'Aldbourne: incised monumental
effigy in the church', *W.N.Q.* 2, 1896-8, 447-52.
Effigy of John Stone, 1501. Also includes
pedigree of Corr, 17th c., with list of creditors of
Anne Corr, 1703.

Wadham

SLADE, J.J. 'A Wiltshirewoman's tomb in
Carisbrooke church', *W.A.M.* 51(182), 1945,
14-17. Lady Margaret Wadham, 17th c.

Washington

GRAY, THOMAS SILL. 'Washington monumental
inscriptions at Garsdon', *Gloucestershire notes
& queries* 2, 1884, 563-5. See also 659-60, & 3,
1887, 535-6.

MANLEY, F.H. 'The Washington memorials at
Garsdon', *W.N.Q.* 6, 1908-10, 481-5; 7, 1911-
13, 1-6, 337-43, 452-7, 481-7 & 529-36.

Webb

REEVES, JOHN. 'A cartouche of Webb arms at Odstock manor house, Wiltshire', *Hatcher review* 2(18), 1984, 382-5. 16-17th c.
'Epitaph of Sir John Webb, 1745', *Notes & queries for Somerset & Dorset* 13, 1913, 113-4. Of Odstock, Wiltshire and Great Canford, Dorset.

10. PROBATE RECORDS AND INQUISITIONS POST MORTEM

A. GENERAL

Probate records—wills, inventories, administration bonds, etc.—are invaluable sources of genealogical information. Wills in particular normally list all surviving children of testators. For Wiltshire, the majority of wills were proved in the Archdeaconry courts of Salisbury (South Wiltshire) and Wiltshire (North Wiltshire), and in the consistory court of Salisbury Diocese. There were also many 'peculiar' jurisdictions. A useful guide to these jurisdictions, although now somewhat out of date, is provided by:

THOMSON, T.R., & RATHBONE, M.G. 'Probate jurisdictions and records for the Diocese of Salisbury', *W.A.M.* 57(206), 1958, 80-83.

Reference should also be made to the works mentioned in *English genealogy: an introductory bibliography*. Section 11.

There are no printed indexes to probate records proved in the major local courts, although Wiltshire Record Office has manuscript indexes. The only index to wills proved locally is provided by:

EVERETT, C.R. 'Wiltshire wills, etc., still preserved in the Diocesan registry, Salisbury', *W.A.M.* 45(152), 1930, 36-67. This covers miscellaneous wills, many of them from the courts of the Dean and Sub-Dean of Salisbury, 1540-1809. It is now incomplete. The records are now at Trowbridge.

An index to Wiltshire wills proved in the Prerogative Court of Canterbury is provided by:

SHELLEY, P.M. 'Wiltshire wills proved in the Prerogative Court of Canterbury', *W.N.Q.* 1, 1893-5, 256-60, 344-52, 393-7, 439-42, 488-9 & 560-62; 2, 1896-8, 65-8 & 111-15; 5, 1905-7, 75-85, 121-8, 180-88, 211-17, 264-72, 313-7, 357-64, 407-16, 455-7 & 521-4; 6, 1908-10, 416-7, 463-6 & 511-15; 7, 1911-13, 21-5, 65-9, 152-7, 275-8, 357-60 & 565-70; 8, 1914-16, 183-6, 323-8, 421-5, 464-71, 519-23 & 538-41.

This is in several sequences, and incomplete. Reference should also be made to the indexes of P.C.C. wills listed in *English genealogy: an introductory bibliography*, section 11.

A small private collection of wills from various courts, 16-18th c., is listed in:

'Copies of wills deposited at W.A.S. library, Devizes', *W.F.H.S.* 16, 1984, 15.

Small collections of probate records from Cliffe Pypard and Semington are edited in:

'Inventories of poor people's furniture at Clyffe Pypard, 1767', *W.A.M.* **48**(168), 1938, 193-6.

SCHOMBERG, ARTHUR. 'Notes on Semington monumental inscriptions', *Genealogist* N.S. **27**, 1911, 105-13. Actually the wills of persons commemorated; see article on monumental inscriptions listed in section 9.

B. BY FAMILY

A number of individual wills have been separately published, as have a number of collections relating to particular families. These are listed here:

Aston
'Simon Aston', *W.N.Q.* **2**, 1896-8, 249. Will, 1638.

Banning
COOK, ALFRed. 'Banning family', *W.N.Q.* **7**, 1911-13, 422-3. Will of John Banning, 1579.

Bayley
'A mayor of Salisbury's will of 1600 A.D. and the advowson of Steeple Langford', *Hatcher review* **2**(12), 1981, 86-91. Will of John Bayley.

Beauchamp
'Anne, Lady Beauchamp's inventory at Edington, Wiltshire, 1665', *W.A.M.* **58**(211), 1963, 383-93.

Benett
'Thomas Benett', *W.N.Q.* **6**, 1908-10, 134-6. See also 183-4. Will, 1558.

Biley
MAY, SAMUEL PEARCE. 'Will of Henry Biley', *New England historical and genealogical register* **42**, 1888, 308-9. Of Salisbury, 1633.

Bisse
WIGAN, HERBERT. 'Bisse notes', *M.G.H.* 3rd series **4**, 1902, 122-9. Includes list of wills proved at Salisbury by the Wiltshire Bisse family, 16-18th c., with a pedigree of Bisse of Almsford, Somerset, etc.

For other works on the Bisse family, see the volume for Somerset in *British genealogical bibliographies*.

Blake
SCHOMBERG, ARTHUR. 'Blake', *W.N.Q.* **1**, 1893-5, 449-54; **4**, 1902-4, 515-7; **5**, 1905-7, 46. Wills, 17-18th c.

Bleobury
'Will of John de Bleobury', *M.G.H.* 5th series **3**, 1918-19, 269-72. 1368.

Bonham
KIDSTON, G.J. 'Some early wills of the Bonham family', *W.A.M.* **48**(169), 1938, 273-91. 14-16th c.

Bower
BOWER, H.B. 'Bower wills, etc.', *M.G.H.* 5th series **7**, 1929-31, 241-3. See also 293 and 326. 16-17th c.

Browne
KITE, EDWARD. 'Wilton House and its literary association', *W.N.Q.* **5**, 1905-7, 528-44. Includes wills of Richard Browne of Calne, 1597, Thomas Moffett, 1604, and Katharine Moffett, 1626.

Budell
CUNNINGTON, B.H. 'Will of Argentina Budell, 8th May 1460', *W.A.M.* **49**(175), 1941, 483-4.

Bundy
'Thomas Bundy's will', *W.N.Q.* **4**, 1902-4, 313-4. 1492.

Chandler
See Le Nhugge

Child
LIGHT, M.E. 'Will of Jonathan Child, Wilts', *W.N.Q.* **3**, 1899-1901, 40-41. 1720.

Edgecombe
HAYCOCK, LORNA. 'The uses of probate inventories to the local historian', *Wiltshire Local History Forum newsletter* **21**, 1992, 4-5. Includes inventory of James Edgecombe of Malmesbury, 1748.

Edington
'William of Edington: founder of Edington Priory, Bishop of Winchester, and first prelate of the most noble order of the Garter', *W.N.Q.* **3**, 1899-1901, 214-21. Will, 1366.

Francklin
'Wiltshire members of the Long Parliament', *W.N.Q.* **1**, 1893-5, 380-1. Despite the title, this is the will of John Francklin of Great Sherston, 1619.

Goddard
GODDARD, RAINALD WM. KNIGHTLEY. 'Goddard of Sedgehill, Co.Wilts', *W.N.Q.* **3**, 1899-1901, 521-5. See also **4**, 1902-4, 171-4. Wills, 16-17th c., with pedigree.

Probate Records etc. *continued*

Goddard *continued*

GODDARD, R.W.K. 'Goddard wills', *M.G.H.* 4th series **2**, 1908, 289-92 & 327-34; **3**, 1910, 6-9, 69-72, 123-6, 162-5, 210-14, 263-7, 293-7 & 360-3; **4**, 1912, 11-15, 85-9, 103-7, 183-90, 231-8 & 252-69. Includes wills from many counties in the South and South-West, including Wiltshire.

GODDARD, RAINALD W. KNIGHTLEY. *Goddard wills.* Mitchell Hughes and Clarke, 1910. Reprinted from *M.G.H.*

GODDARD, RAINALD WILLIAM KNIGHTLEY. 'Goddard family', *Fragmenta Genealogica* **7**, 1902, 73-102. Of Wiltshire, Berkshire, and various other counties. Wills, 15-17th c .

Grobham

'Will of Sir Richard Grobham, A.D. 1628', *W.N.Q.* **5**, 1905-7, 32-9.

Hayne

HAYNES, D.F. 'Will of Alice Hayne, 1620, of Semley, Eng', *New England historical and genealogical register* **39**, 1885, 263-4.

Holes

'The will of Andrew Holes, A.D. 1470', *W.N.Q.* **4**, 1902-4, 566-71.

Horton

KITE, E. 'Horton wills', *W.N.Q.* **4**, 1902-4, 163-70. Includes pedigree, 16th c.

Houlton

BOUCHER, R. 'Houlton-Selfe', *W.N.Q.* **4**, 1902-4, 416-7. Wills of John and Jane Houlton of Bradford, 1681-2.

Huddesfeld

R., C.S. 'John Huddesfeld', *W.N.Q.* **4**, 1902-4, 69-72. 1545.

Hungerford

B., G. 'Abstracts of Hungerford wills', *Collectanea topographica et genealogica* **7**, 1841, 70-72. 15-16th c.

Jacob

P., W. 'Will of Thomas Jacob of Wootton Bassett', *W.N.Q.* **4**, 1902-4, 469-72. 1644.

King

MORRISON, GEORGE AUSTIN. 'Richard King, 1616-1668', *Notes & queries for Somerset & Dorset* **12**, 1911, 261-5 & 293-6. See also 211. Includes King wills from Wiltshire, Oxfordshire and Berkshire.

Lambert

'The will of Thomas Lambert, Canon of Salisbury, and Archdeacon of Wilts, 1674', *W.A.M.* **47**(163), 1935, 272-4.

Langford

'Hyde and Langford of Trowbridge', *W.N.Q.* **1**, 1893-5, 519-21. Wills of Langford family, 16-17th c.

Le Nhugge

SMITH, WILLIAM. 'Two medieval Salisbury wills', *Journal of the Society of Archivists* **10**(3), 1989, 118-22. Wills of John Le Nhugge, 1332-3, and John Chandler, 1406.

Lisle

BAKER, H. DE FOE. 'The will of Lady Mary Lisle, A.D. 1524', *Transactions of the Salisbury Field Club* **1**, 1890-91, 172-4.

Longespee

MALDEN, A.R. 'The will of Nicholas Longespee, Bishop of Salisbury', *English historical review* **15**, 1900, 523-8. 1297.

Ludlow

SCHOMBERG, A. 'Will of John Ludlow', *W.N.Q.* **7**, 1911-13, 423-4. 1519.

Michell

'Will of Samuel Michell of Notton, 1694', *W.N.Q.* **6**, 1908-10, 269-70.

Moffett

See Browne

Newton

'Will of John Newton', *W.N.Q.* **7**, 1911-13, 167-70. 1477.

Nicholas

SCHOMBERG, ARTHUR. 'Robert Nicholas', *W.N.Q.* **1**, 1893-5, 321-3. Will, 1667.

Norton

'Will of John Norton', *W.N.Q.* **8**, 1914-16, 321-3. 1402.

Panton

'Panton and Selfe', *W.N.Q.* **4**, 1902-4, 572-3. Will of Cecilia Panton, 1744.

Pleydell

'Edington', *W.N.Q.* **5**, 1905-7, 88-91 & 129-36. Wills and deeds concerning Pleydell family, 16-17th c.

Polton

SOAMES, C. 'The will of Thomas Polton, Bishop of Worcester, A.D. 1432', *W.A.M.* **26**(76), 1892, 52-83.

Raleigh

'The Society's mss. inventory of the goods of Sir Charles Raleigh, of Downton, 1698', *W.A.M.* **42**(139), 1923, 307-12.

Rede

WHITLEY, W.T., ed. 'Devizes in 1699', *Baptist Quarterly* **9**(3), 1938, 164-5. Text of bequest by John Rede of Porton to Baptist ministers.

Richmond

RICHMOND, HENRY I. 'Richmond alias Webb', *M.G.H.* 5th series **7**, 1929-31, 84-7 & 109-13. Wills, mainly from Wiltshire and Berkshire, 16-18th c.

Rolfe

See Whittier

Savage

HORTON-SMITH, L.G.H. 'The family of Savage of Co.Wilts', *W.A.M.* **50**(180), 1944, 309-32. 17-18th c., includes list of probate records, etc.

Scull

SCULL, G.D. 'Abstracts of wills relating to the family of Scull or Skull', *M.G.H.* N.S. **2**, 1877, 277-9. 17th c.

Spencer

See Thorner

Stokes

'Stokes', *M.G.H.* 3rd series **2**, 1898, 133. Wills of John Stokes, 1498, and John Stokes, 1664, both of Seend.

Stone

'Will of John Stone', *W.N.Q.* **8**, 1914-16, 537-8. 1524.

Thorner

POYNTON, F.J. 'Evidences supporting the genealogies of Thorner, White and Spencer of Wilts', *M.G.H.* 2nd series **1**, 1886, 134-9 & 149-52. Wills, 17-18th c., also extracts from parish registers of Malmesbury and Great Somerford.

Tooke

'Will of Jane Tooke, widow, late wife of Walter Tooke, deceased: will P.C.C. 107 Dale', *W.A.M.* **50**(177), 1942, 106-7. 1620.

Trenchard

SAGE. 'Trenchard', *W.N.Q.* **4**, 1902-4, 177. Will of Francis Trenchard, of Normanton, 1635.

SCHOMBERG, A. 'Trenchard wills', *W.N.Q.* **4**, 1902-4, 325-30. See also 283. 16-17th c.

Trye

KITE, EDWARD. 'Will of Joan Trye, [1533], mother of the last abbess of Lacock', *W.N.Q.* **6**, 1908-10, 554-62. See also 7, 1911-13, 57-9.

Walrond

DUNLOP, J. RENTON. 'Walrond', *M.G.H.* 5th series **4**, 1920-22, 262. Will of Thomas Walrond of Little Hinton, 1597/8.

Waltham

KITE, EDWARD. 'Will of John de Waltham, Bishop of Salisbury', *W.N.Q.* **6**, 1908-10, 438-44. Born at Waltham, Lincolnshire; will dated 1395.

Webb

See Richmond

White

See Thorner

Whittier

WHITTIER, CHARLES COLLYER. *Notes on the English ancestry of Whittier and Rolfe families of New England*. Boston: [ ], 1912. Reprinted from *New England historical and genealogical register*. Includes wills and extracts from Wiltshire parish registers, with brief 16-17th c. pedigree.

Willis

'Thomas Willis, M.D.', *W.N.Q.* **8**, 1914-16, 337-42. Includes will, 1675.

Writh

'Will of John Writh, Garter King of Arms', *W.N.Q.* **7**, 1911-13, 448-50. 1504. Name subsequently changed to Wriothesley.

C. *INQUISITIONS POST MORTEM*

Inquisitions post mortem are invaluable sources of genealogical information for the medieval period (to the 1640s) and are particularly useful in tracing the descent of manors. For Wiltshire abstracts, see:

FRY, EDW. ALEX., ed. *Abstracts of Wiltshire inquisitions post mortem returned into the Court of Chancery in the reigns of Henry III, Edward I, and Edward II, A.D. 1242-1326.* Index Library **37**. British Record Society, 1908.

STOKES, ETHEL, ed. *Abstracts of Wiltshire inquisitions post mortem returned into the Court of Chancery in the reign of King Edward III, A.D. 1327-1377.* Index Library **48.** British Record Society, 1914.

FRY, GEORGE S., & FRY, EDWARD ALEXANDER. *Abstracts of Wiltshire inquisitions post mortem returned into the Court of Chancery in the reign of King Charles the First.* Index Library **23.** British Record Society and W.A.N.H.S. Records Branch, 1901.

11. OFFICIAL LISTS OF NAMES

Governments like to know who is subject to their jurisdiction, so that they can tax them, insist on their loyalty, require them to undertake military service, allow them to vote, and a whole host of other reasons. The compilation of lists of people has been a vital administrative activity for centuries, and genealogists have cause to be thankful for the ever extending range of activities for which lists have been needed. The earliest such list is, of course, Domesday book, which identifies manorial lords; an easily accessible edition is provided by:

THORN, CAROLINE & FRANK, eds. *Domesday book, 6: Wiltshire.* Chichester: Phillimore, 1976. An edition is also provided in the *Victoria County History* (see section 1 above).

Tax Lists

For Wiltshire, the only major printed tax lists covering the whole county to be printed are the subsidy rolls of 1332 and 1576, and the benevolence of 1545:

CROWLEY, D.A. *The Wiltshire tax list of 1332.* W.R.S. **45,** 1989.

RAMSAY, G.D., ed. *Two sixteenth century taxation lists, 1545 and 1576.* W.R.S. **10,** 1954.

A number of briefer tax lists from particular hundreds, deaneries, etc., have been published, and are listed here chronologically:

CAZEL, FRED A., & CAZEL, ANNARIE P., eds. *Rolls of the fifteenth of the ninth year of the reign of Henry III for Cambridgeshire, Lincolnshire and Wiltshire, and rolls of the fortieth of the seventeenth year of the reign of Henry III for Kent.* Publications of the Pipe Roll Society, **83;** N.S. **45,** 1983 (for 1976-77). Wiltshire portion comprises the clergy returns for the Deanery of Chalke only.

KIRBY, J.L., ed. 'Clerical poll-taxes in the Diocese of Salisbury, 1377-81', in WILLIAMS, N.J., ed. *Collectanea.* W.R.S. **12,** 1956, 157-67.

WORDSWORTH, CHR. 'Marlborough poll tax, 1379', *W.N.Q.* **6,** 1908-10, 535-46.

PUGH, C.W. 'Ship-money in the Hundred of Kingsbridge', *W.A.M.* **50**(178), 1943, 153-69. Tax list, 1635.

'Copy of a ms. in the possession of Sir Walter Grove, Baronet, to which is prefixed a copy of a lay subsidy preserved in the Public Record Office', *W.A.M.* **38**(122), 1914, 589-630. Dunworth Hundred, subsidy roll, 1641.

'Return for the Hundred of Westbury, 1643', *W.A.M.* **39**(126), 1917, 445-8. Tax list.

49

BAKER, T.H. 'The monthly assessments for the relief of Ireland raised in the Division of Warminster', *W.A.M.* **37**(117), 1912, 353-79.

NEVILL, EDMUND R. 'Salisbury: a royal aid and supply for 1667', *W.A.M.* **36**(113), 1910, 413-34.

Muster rolls

The defence of the realm necessitated the compilation of lists of those liable to serve. There is no modern edition of a Wiltshire muster roll; however, an edition was printed in the early 19th century (although it is now very rare).

[PHILLIPPS], SIR T., ed. *North Wiltshire musters, anno, 30 Henry VIII, from the original in the Chapter House, Westminster.* T. Gardiner & Son, 1834. I have not seen this.

Loyalty Oaths

Another type of official list resulted from the clash of loyalties at the beginning of the Great Rebellion. The House of Commons demanded an oath of loyalty from all subjects of the crown; the result, now to be seen in the House of Lords Record Office, was the 'protestation' returns of 1641/2, which contain the signatures of most adult males in the great majority of English parishes. Those for Wiltshire are printed in:

FRY, E.A. 'Wiltshire protestation returns of 1641-2', *W.N.Q.* **7**, 1911-13, 16-21, 79-84, 105-10, 162-7, 203-8, 260-65, 309-13, 343-7, 418-21, 450-52 & 496-9.

The coming of the House of Orange led in 1696 to the taking of another 'oath of loyalty'. Wiltshire signatories to the Association oath are listed in:

PILE, L.J. ACTON. 'Association oath rolls for Wiltshire', *W.N.Q.* **6**, 1908-10, 197-201, 349-51 & 485-92. See also **7**, 1911-13, 42-43.

Poll Books

As the eighteenth century developed, loyalty of another kind came to be increasingly recorded. The earliest poll-book for a Wiltshire parliamentary election is dated 1705. Poll books list those claiming the right to vote, and sometimes also indicate how they cast their vote. Poll books for the county exist for 1705, 1772, 1818, 1819, 1833 and 1837. There are also poll books—mainly nineteenth century—for South Wiltshire, Chippenham, Cricklade, Devizes, Malmesbury, Salisbury, and Wootton Bassett. After 1832, electoral registers were also prepared officially. Details of these, and the location of the (few) surviving copies, are given in the works listed in *English genealogy: an introductory bibliography*, section 12, D. The only other work on Wiltshire poll books to be published is:

LIGHT, M.E. 'A poll of Wiltshire in 1705', *W.N.Q.* **1**, 1893-5, 368-70. See also 418.

See also:

OBSERVER. *Kaleidoscopiana Wiltoniensia, or, a literary, political and moral view of the county of Wilts during the contested election ... June 1818 ... containing the whole of the advertisements, letters, speeches, squibs and songs ...* J. Brettell, 1818. Fascinating account of a 19th c. election. For the genealogist, it contains many names.

Census Returns

By far the most useful 'official lists' are those derived from the official censuses. These began in 1801, but normally the earliest surviving returns of genealogical value are for 1841. For Wiltshire, however, there is an unofficial census for Chisledon dated 1787, and what appears to be the list compiled by the official census enumerator for Woodborough in 1811. These have both been published in *W.F.H.S.*, as have the official returns from a number of Wiltshire parishes for later censuses—and also a few lists of Wiltshire migrants found in census returns from other counties. The following list is in chronological order:

1787

HURLEY, BERYL. 'A list of the inhabitants of the parish of Chisledon, Feb 15th, 1787', *W.F.H.S.* **35**, 1989, 33-4 & **36**, 1990, 14-16.

1811

TRACE, MARY KEARNS. 'The population of Woodborough in 1811', *W.F.H.S.* **34**, 1989, 19. List of heads of households with numbers in families, found pasted in the front cover of the parish register.

1841

METHERELL, BERYL. 'Index of names in 1841 census of Chisledon, Wiltshire', *W.F.H.S.* **2**, 1981, 10-16.

1851

'Index of names appearing in 1851 census of Alton Barnes, Wiltshire', *W.F.H.S.* **3**, 1981, 12-13.

CHAMPION, BRIAN. 'Wilts strays in West Bromwich', *W.F.H.S.* **37**, 1990, 31 & **38**, 1990, 10. Staffordshire; from the 1851 census.

'List of surnames of persons born in Wiltshire who appear in the 1851 census of Marshfield, Gloucestershire', *W.F.H.S.* **5**, 1982, 16.

'Far from home', *W.F.H.S.* **29**, 1988, 16-17. Wiltshire entries in the 1851 census returns for Neath, Glamorganshire.

MARSH, ROBERT. 'Index of names appearing in 1851 census of Stanton St.Bernard, Wiltshire', *W.F.H.S.* **3**, 1981, 10-12.

1861

'Servants in training in Calne: Calne 1861 census: Training Institution for Servants in Curzon Street, Calne', *W.F.H.S.* **35**, 1989, 25.

1881

The Mormons are currently preparing a full index to the 1881 census. When this is complete, it will be an essential tool for all genealogists.

'Swindon census, 1881, roll 1406: persons attending Swindon fair and sleeping in carts or sleeping rough', *W.F.H.S.* **1**, 1983, 25-6.

'1881 census: parish of Eling, Hants', *W.F.H.S.* **33**, 1989, 14. Lists Wiltshire names.

HULBERT, CHRIS. 'List of surnames of persons born in Wiltshire who appear in the 1881 census of Marshfield, Glos', *W.F.H.S.* **10**, 1983, 31.

COWARD, P.E. 'List of surnames of Wiltshire-born persons appearing in the 1881 census for Poole, Dorset', *W.F.H.S.* **20**, 1986, 22.

Landowners Census

A census of a different kind was taken in 1873. The *Return of owners of land* records the names of everyone who owned an acre or more of land. See:

Return of owners of land, 1873: Wilts. House of Commons Parliamentary papers, 1874, 72, pt.2, 503-31.

12. DIRECTORIES AND MAPS

Directories are an invaluable source of information for locating people in the past. For the nineteenth century, they are the equivalent of the modern phone book. Many directories for Wiltshire were published; the list which follows is selective, largely based on volumes actually seen in Trowbridge and London, although also drawing on information from the works listed in section 13 of *English genealogy: an introductory bibliography*. Directories usually have a short life, and consequently, 19th c. examples tend to be rare; in some cases, it is possible that there were earlier or later editions than those noted below, but which I have been unable to trace. This list is in chronological order. Late 20th century directories are not listed.

TUNNICLIFF, WILL. *A topographical survey of the counties of Hants, Wilts, Dorset, Somerset, Devon & Cornwall.* Salisbury: B.C. Collins, 1791.

The Wiltshire register for 182-. Melksham: J. Cockrane, 1825-6. 2 issues. Includes various lists of officials, etc., e.g. justices of the peace, clergy, councillors, postmasters.

Hunt & Co's directory and court guide for the cities of Bath, Bristol & Wells, and the towns of Bradford, Calne, Chippenham, Devizes, Frome, Lavingtons, Melksham, Shepton Mallet, Trowbridge, Warminster & Westbury ... E. Hunt & Co., 1848. Wells, Frome and Shepton Mallet are in Somerset, as was Bath.

Kelly's directory of Wiltshire. Kelly & Co., 1848-1939. 19 issues. Variously titled; frequently published in conjunction with directories for neighbouring counties, e.g. *Kelly's directory of Hampshire, Wiltshire and Dorsetshire, including the Isle of Wight.* Alternative title: *Post Office directory ...*

Hunt & Co's directory of Dorsetshire, with parts of Hants and Wilts ... 1851. E. Hunt & Co., 1851.

J.G. Harrod & Co's postal and commercial directory of Wiltshire. J.G. Harrod & Co., 1865.

W.E. Owen & Co's general, topographical and historical directory for the counties of Wiltshire, Somersetshire, with the cities of Bristol and Bath. Leicester: W.E. Owen & Co., 1878.

W.E. Owen & Co's general, topographical and historical directory for Gloucestershire, Wiltshire, Somersetshire, Monmouthshire, Radnorshire, with the cities of Bristol and Bath. Leicester: W.E. Owen, 1879.

Directories and Maps continued

Deacon's court guide gazetteer and royal blue book embracing with the whole of the towns in the western division of Gloucestershire, Chippenham, Devizes, Frome, Marlborough, Shepton Mallet, Swindon, Trowbridge, Yeovil, and the cities of Salisbury, Gloucester, Bristol, Bath & Wells. 2nd ed. C.W. Deacon & Co., 1882.

Somersetshire, Dorsetshire and Wiltshire directory. Walsall: Aubrey & Co., 1909-41. 6 issues.

Somersetshire, Dorsetshire and Wiltshire directory. Walsall: Aubrey & Co., 1935-7.

Bradford on Avon

The Bradford-on-Avon annual, household almanack, directory, and advertiser. Bradford on Avon: Charles Rawling, 1869-95. 8 issues.

Dotesio's illustrated commercial diary, almanack and directory. Bradford-on-Avon: W. Dotesio, 1894-1914. 14 issues. For Bradford on Avon. Earlier issues do not include directory.

Calne

Heath's directory and almanack for Calne and neighbourhood ... Calne: Heath, 1888-1930. 10 issues.

Chippenham

Spinke's Chippenham almanac and directory. Chippenham: S. Spinke, 1877-1957. Almost annual.

Directory of Chippenham and district. Chippenham Chamber of Commerce, 1939.

Devizes

Gillman's Devizes public register, business directory, and family almanack. Devizes: C. Gillman, 1858-1933. Annual from 1863. Continued as *Devizes & District almanack & directory.* Devizes: Wiltshire gazette, 1934-9 and 1947-58.

Highworth

Smith's Highworth almanac, diary and directory. Highworth: J.J. Smith, 1888.

Malmesbury

Harmer's Cotswold almanack and trade directory for 1868, comprising the calendar, a guide and directory for Cirencester, Fairford, Cricklade, Lechlade, Tetbury, Malmesbury and Northleach. Cirencester: H. Harmer, 1868-9. Cricklade and Malmesbury are in Wiltshire; the other places are in Gloucestershire.

Taylors directory: Malmesbury, Cirencester and district, Purton, Cricklade, Wootton Bassett, and all surrounding villages. Swindon: Taylors, 1890-1941. Cirencester is in Gloucestershire.

Riddick's directory of Malmesbury and adjoining villages. Malmesbury: J. Riddick, 1910-39. 12 issues.

Marlborough

Lucy's Marlborough and District directory. Marlborough: Lucy & Co., 1874?-1934. Annual from 1906. Continued by: *The Marlborough and District directory.* Marlborough: W. Gale, 1937-53.

Salisbury

A directory of the city of Salisbury and surrounding districts. Salisbury: F. Mundy & Co., 1891.

Brown's directory of Salisbury. Salisbury: Brown & Co., 1906-16. Almost annual. Continued by: *Directory of Salisbury and the neighbourhood.* Salisbury: Salisbury & District Chamber of Commerce, 1923-5. 2 issues. Continued by: *Kelly's directory of Salisbury and the neighbourhood.* Kelly's Directories, 1927-. Almost bi-annual.

Directory of Salisbury and District. Salisbury: Langmead & Evans, 1897/8-1908. Annual.

Swindon

The Swindon and District illustrated almanack and directory. Swindon: North Wilts Herald, 1875-8. 3 issues.

Astill & Co's original Swindon almanack and directory. Swindon: R. Astill & Co., 1877-8. 2 issues. Other editions do not include the directory section. Continued by: *The North Wilts, Borough of Cricklade & District directory.* Swindon: North Wilts Herald, 1879-1923. Annual. Title varies. Continued by: *The Swindon and District directory and year book.* Swindon: Swindon Press, 1924-53. Annual except for 1941-6.

Trowbridge

The Trowbridge household almanack, directory and general advertiser. Trowbridge: B. Harris, 1859.

Collins almanack and directory of Trowbridge and neighbourhood. Trowbridge: W. Collins, 1888-1907. 15 issues. Continued by *Collins almanack and West Wilts directory, including Trowbridge, Westbury, Melksham, Warminster, Bradford on Avon, and villages.* B. Lansdown & Sons, 1908-57. Annual; title varies.

Directories and Maps continued

Trowbridge continued

Coleman's Trowbridge, Bradford and Westbury directories. Trowbridge: George Coleman, 1906-8. Annual.

Warminster

The Warminster and district directory and almanack. Warminster: Coates & Parker, 1914-1939. 4 issues.

Westbury

Westbury directory. Westbury: A.E. & H. Holloway, 1935-40. 4 issues.

Maps

Directories sometimes, usefully, include maps, which you will need to consult in order to locate particular places. Early maps reveal a great deal about the way in which the landscape has changed in modern times. Two have been reprinted in book form:

Andrews' and Dury's map of Wiltshire, 1773: a reduced facsimile. W.A.N.H.S. Records Branch 8, 1952.

The old series Ordnance Survey maps of England and Wales ... vol.3. Central England; vol.4. South-Central England. Lympne Castle: Harry Margary, 1981-6.

Individual sheet maps of the 1st edition 1" Ordnance Survey have been reprinted by the publishers David & Charles.

Many early maps are listed in:

CHUBB, T. 'A descriptive catalogue of the printed maps of Wiltshire from 1576 to the publication of the 25 in. Ordnance Survey, 1885', W.A.M. 37(116), 1911, 211-326.

BELL, W. HEWARD, AND GODDARD, E.H. Catalogue of the collection of drawings, prints and maps in the library of the Wiltshire Archaeological and Natural History Society, at Devizes. Devizes: C.H. Woodward, 1898.

For maps of historic Salisbury, see:

LOBEL, M.D., ed. Historic towns: maps and plans of towns and cities in the British Isles, with historical commentaries, from earliest times to 1800, vol. 1. Lovell Johns-Cook, Hammond & Kell Organization, 1969.

Reference must also be made to the sheet parish map of Wiltshire issued by the Institute of Heraldic and Genealogical Studies, which is an essential tool for every Wiltshire genealogist.

Place Names

To identify those obscure place-names which you will often find in genealogical sources, consult:

GOVER, J.E.G., MAWER, ALLEN, & STENTON, F.M. The place-names of Wiltshire. English Place-Name Society 16. Cambridge: Cambridge U.P., 1939.

More up to date, but less comprehensive, is:

TOMKINS, RICHARD. Wiltshire place names. Swindon: Redbrick Publishing, 1983.

Dialect

You may also come across dialect words that you do not understand. For these, consult:

AKERMAN, J.Y. A glossary of provincial words and phrases in use in Wiltshire. John Russell Smith, 1842.

DARTNELL, GEORGE EDWARD, AND GODDARD, EDWARD HUNGERFORD. A glossary of words used in the county of Wiltshire. Oxford University Press for the English Dialect Society, 1893. Reprinted with introduction by Norman Rogers. Avebury: Wiltshire Life Society, 1991. Reprint includes addenda originally printed as:

GODDARD, C.V., AND E.H. 'Wiltshire words: addenda', W.A.M. 46(160), 1934, 478-519.

13. RELIGIOUS RECORDS

The church played a much greater role in pre-industrial society than it does today. Consequently, many of the records essential to the genealogist are to be found in ecclesiastical rather than state archives—for example, parish registers, probate records, parochial records, etc. Works on ecclesiastical sources are to be found throughout this bibliography; this section concentrates on those topics which are primarily to do with the administration of the church. The best introduction to the history of the church in Wiltshire is provided by the *Victoria County History* (see section 1). Another valuable introduction to the history of churches in South East Wiltshire is provided by a recent account of its architecture:

ROYAL COMMISSION ON THE HISTORICAL MONUMENTS OF ENGLAND. *Churches of South-East Wiltshire.* H.M.S.O., 1987. The authoritative study. Includes a few notes on monumental inscriptions; has a useful bibliography.

Biographies of the bishops of Salisbury are presented in:

CASSAN, S.H. *Lives and memoirs of the Bishops of Sherborne and Salisbury, from the year 705 to 1824.* Salisbury: Brodie & Dowding, 1824.

For the records of the Diocese, see:

STEWART, PAMELA. *Diocese of Salisbury: guide to the records of the Bishop, the Archdeacons of Salisbury and Wiltshire, and other Archidiaconal and peculiar jurisdictions, and to the records from the Bishop of Bristol's Sub-Registry for Dorset.* Wiltshire County Council guide to the record offices 4. Bradford on Avon: the Council, 1973.

POOLE, REGINALD L. 'The records of the Bishop of Salisbury', in HISTORICAL MANUSCRIPTS COMMISSION *Report on manuscripts in various collections* 4. Cd.3218. H.M.S.O., 1907, 1-12.
'The records of the Bishop of Salisbury', in HISTORICAL MANUSCRIPTS COMMISSION *Seventeenth report ...* Cd.3737. H.M.S.O., 1907, 109-12.

POOLE, REGINALD L. 'The muniments of the Dean and Chapter of Salisbury', in HISTORICAL MANUSCRIPTS COMMISSION *Report on manuscripts in various collections* 1. Cd.784. H.M.S.O., 1901, 338-88.

SMITH, WILLIAM. 'A select account of the private papers of Bishop Seth Ward in the Wiltshire Record Office', *W.A.M.* 76, 1982, 115-22.

For works dealing with the Diocesan Record Office, see section 2B.

The most important ecclesiastical sources for the medieval period are the bishops registers, which record the general business of the diocese. The lists of ordinations and institutions they contain, together with the occasional will, are of particular genealogical value. Published medieval registers etc. include:

JONES, W.H. RICH. *Charters and documents illustrating the history of the cathedral, city and diocese of Salisbury in the twelfth and thirteenth centuries selected from the capitular and diocesan registers.* ed. W. Dunn Macray. Rolls series 97. H.M.S.O., 1891.

JONES, W.H.R., ed. *Vetus registrum Sarisberiense, alias dictum registrum S. Osmundi episcopi/the register of S. Osmund.* 2 vols. Rolls series 78. H.M.S.O., 1883-4.

FLOWER, C.T., AND DAWES, M.C.B. *Registrum Simonis de Gandavo: Diocesis Saresbiriensis A.D. 1297-1315.* 2 vols. Canterbury and York Society, 40-41. 1934.

EDWARDS, KATHLEEN, ed. *The registers of Roger Martival, Bishop of Salisbury 1315-1330.* Canterbury and York Society, 55, 57-9 and 68. Oxford: O.U.P., 1959-75. v.1. The register of presentations and institutions to benefices. v.2. The register of divers letters. v.3. Royal writs. v.4. General introduction, and The register of inhibitions and acts, ed. Dorothy M. Owen.

CHEW, HELENA M., ed. *Hemingby's register.* W.R.S. 18, 1963. Salisbury Cathedral chapter act book, 1329-49; includes detailed biographical notes.

TIMMINS, T.C.B., ed. *The register of John Chandler, Dean of Salisbury, 1404-17.* W.R.S. 39, 1984.

HORN, JOYCE M., ed. *The register of Robert Hallum, Bishop of Salisbury 1407-17.* Canterbury and York Society 72, 1982.

WRIGHT, D.P., ed. *The register of Thomas Langton, Bishop of Salisbury, 1485-93.* Canterbury and York Society 74, 1985.

Witnesses in the Dean's Consistory Court, 1597-9, with their residences, occupations and ages, are listed in:

EVERETT, C.R. 'Sarum diocesan court records, 1597-9', *Genealogists magazine* 7, 1935-7, 182-5.

Many lists of Wiltshire clergy have been printed. The standard guide to senior clergy in the Diocese of Salisbury is:

Religious Records *continued*

LE NEVE, JOHN. *Fasti ecclesiae Anglicanae 1300-1541, III: Salisbury Diocese*, comp. Joyce M. Horn. Athlone Press, 1962.

LE NEVE, JOHN. *Fasti ecclesiae Anglicanae, 1541-1857, VI: Salisbury Diocese*, comp. Joyce M. Horn. Institute of Historical Research, 1986.

This largely replaces:

JONES, W.H. *Fasti ecclesiae Sarisberiensis, or a calendar of the bishops, deans, archdeacons, and members of the Cathedral body at Salisbury, from the earliest times to the present.* Salisbury: Brown & Co.; London: Simpkin Marshall & Co., 1879.

Institutions to livings are listed in:

PHILLIPPS, THOMAS, ed. *Institutiones clericorum in comitatu Wiltoniae ab anno 1297 ad annum 1810.* 2 vols. [Middle Hill]: Typis Medio-Montanis, 1825. Indexed in: JACKSON, J.E. 'Index to the *Wiltshire institutions* as printed by Sir Thomas Phillipps', *W.A.M.* **28**, 1896, 210-35.

Many Wiltshire advowsons (i.e. the right of presentation to ecclesiastical livings) were owned by the Duchy of Lancaster. Fifteenth century presentations of clergy by the Duchy are listed in: *Notes from the rolls of the chancery of the Duchy of Lancaster relating to Wiltshire'*, W.N.Q. **7**, 1911-13, 257-60.

Other lists of clergy include (in chronological order):

PALMER, C.F.R. 'The Black Friars of Wiltshire", *W.A.M.* **18**(53), 1874, 162-76. Includes list of friars and tenants at the dissolution.

CLARK, W. GILCHRIST. 'The fall of the Wiltshire monasteries", *W.A.M.* **28**(85), 1896, 288-319. Includes lists of pensions assigned to former monks.

WILLIAMS, BARRIE, ed. *The subscription book of Bishop"s Tounson and Davenant, 1620-40.* W.R.S. **32**, 1977. Recording subscriptions of clergy to the 39 Articles.

'Wilts parochial clergy sufferers under the Usurpation, (1642-61)", *W.N.Q.* **8**, 1914-16, 506-14. Alphabetical list.

WORDSWORTH, CHR. 'Wilts ministers (1643-1662)", *W.A.M.* **34**, 1905, 159-92 and 243-5. Various lists of clergy.

JONES, W.H. 'Register of church livings in Wilts, in the time of the Commonwealth (A.D. 1645-1650)", *W.A.M.* **19**(56), 1881, 182-216. Lists patrons and incumbents.

BODINGTON, E.J. 'The church survey in Wilts., 1649-50", *W.A.M.* **40**, 1919, 253-72, 297-317 392-416; **41**, 1922, 1-39 & 105-28. Gives names of many ministers, churchwardens, etc.

EVERETT, C.R. 'The Act of Uniformity, 1662: declaration by ministers (of Salisbury Diocese)", *W.A.M.* **45**(155), 1931, 477-82. Includes signatures of over 250 clergy.

'Ministers in the Malmesbury District about the time of the civil wars and Restoration", *W.N.Q.* **7**, 1911-13, 546-51. Brief biographical notes.

MANLEY, F.H. 'A subscription book of the Deans of Sarum (1662-1706)", *W.A.M.* **46**(159), 1933, 356-60. Description of book containing many signatures—but the latter are not printed.

RANSOME, MARY, ed. *Wiltshire returns to the bishop"s visitation queries, 1783.* W.R.S. **27**, 1972. Amongst much else, gives names of clergy, etc.

Many histories of particular churches have been compiled, and frequently include clergy lists, the names of churchwardens, parish register extracts, monumental inscriptions, etc. These cannot be listed here; you should check the bibliographies listed in section 2, or ask one of the libraries listed on page 5 what is available. Lists of clergy in particular places, together with other miscellaneous information, are provided by:

Box

IBBERSON, DAVID. *The vicars of St.Thomas a Becket, Box: their lives and times.* Corsham: Addkey Print, 1987. Includes pedigrees of Webb, 16-17th c., and Horlock, 19-20th c.

Great Bedwin

W., J. 'Account of the church of Bedwyn Magna in Wiltshire, with a list of the vicars, and extracts from the parish registers, and others from Bedwyn Parva, Frosfield and Easton", *Collectanea topographica et genealogica* **5**, 1838, 20-40. Includes monumental inscriptions.

Malmesbury

BIRCH, W. DE G. 'On the succession of the abbots of Malmesbury", *Journal of the British Archaeological Association* **27**, 1871, 314-42. List of abbots, with biographical notes. Also includes notes on the abbey"s records.

Marlborough

WORDSWORTH, CHR. 'Marlborough chantries and the supply of clergy in olden days", *W.A.M.* **36**(114), 1910, 525-84. Includes list of chaplains, extracts from wills, deeds, etc.

Religious Records continued

Rowde

SCRIBA. 'List of incumbents from the parish register of Rowde", *W.N.Q.* **8**, 1914-16, 21-3.

Religious Records continued

Salisbury Cathedral

MOOR, C. 'Cardinals beneficed in Sarum Cathedral', *W.A.M.* **50**(178), 1943, 136-48. Includes biographical notes.

Salisbury. St.Thomas

NEVILL, EDMUND R. 'The Chrysom book of St.Thomas, Salisbury", *W.N.Q.* **5**, 1902-5, 462-8, 510-14 & 561-6; **6**, 1908-10, 19-25, 57-60, 107-10, 176-9, 208-11, 266-8, 302-5, 344-8, 391-5, 455-9, 492-8 & 547-50. Lists those making offerings at christenings and marriages, 1569-92.

Trowbridge

PITT, F.C. *The parish church of St.James, Trowbridge: a brief historical and descriptive guide.* Trowbridge: B. Lansdown & Sons, 1932. Includes list of rectors, and some notes on monuments.

Warminster

COLEMAN, PREBENDARY. 'The prebend and prebendaries of Warminster, alias Luxvile, in the Cathedral church of Wells", *Somerset Archaeological and Natural History Society transactions* **47**(2), 1901, 189-216.

Wilton

NIGHTINGALE, J.E. 'On the succession of the abbesses of Wilton, with some notice of Wilton seals", *W.A.M.* **19**(57), 1881, 342-62.

Wroughton

MASKELYNE, T. STORY, AND MANLEY, CANON. 'Notes on the ecclesiastical history of Wroughton, its rectors and vicars", *W.A.M.* **41**(136), 1922, 451-78. Includes list of clergy.

Nonconformists

Many different denominations have been active in Wiltshire, their register of baptisms, marriages and burials are listed in section 8. For a valuable architectural introduction to Wiltshire nonconformity, see:

STELL, CHRISTOPHER. *An inventory of nonconformist chapels and meeting-houses in South-West England.* H.M.S.O., 1991. Includes a useful list of Wiltshire nonconformist chapels, with some notes on monumental inscriptions.

Nonconformists continued

A number of works provide names of nonconformist clergy and lay people:

SCHOMBERG, A. 'Wiltshire nonconformists, 1662", *W.N.Q.* **8**, 1914-16, 12-16, 152-5, 357-69 & 396-8. List of ministers ejected at the Restoration.

DORAN-WEBB, EDWARD. 'Conventicles in Sarum Diocese, A.D. 1669", *Transactions of the Salisbury Field Club* **1**, 1890-1, 36-46. Gives names of nonconformists.

CHANDLER, J.H., ed. *Wiltshire dissenters" meeting house certificates and registrations, 1689-1852.* W.R.S., **40**, 1985. Gives names on c.1800 certificates.

Baptists

COOPER, F.W. *The Wilts and East Somerset Association of Baptist churches, 1862-1976.* Yeovil: the Association, 1975. Includes lists of churches and officers.

Bradford on Avon

OLIVER, ROBERT W. *Baptists in Bradford on Avon: the history of the Old Baptist Church, Bradford on Avon, 1689-1989.* Bradford on Avon: Old Baptist Chapel, 1989. Includes much information on pastors, and on leading members.

Bratton

REEVES, E.S.W., K., & M. *1662-1962: a history of the Baptist Church, Bratton, Wilts.* Paulton: Durham West & Sons, 1962. Includes lists of ministers and deacons.

Devizes

HURLEY, JOHN. 'Baptist records", *W.F.H.S.* **30**, 1988, 26-7. General discussion, with some 19th c. extracts from Devizes New Baptist church.

HURLEY, BERYL, & JOHN. *The new Baptist Church, Devizes: brief history and membership book, 1805-1945.* W.F.H.S., 1991.

Melksham

COOPER, F.W. *Broughton Road Baptist Church, Melksham: a short history.* Shoreham by Sea: Service Publications, c.1969. Includes lists of clergy and officers, with calendar of church archives.

North Bradley

ISAACS, A.P. *The Baptists at North Bradley since 1650.* Trowbridge: Actionprint, 1982. Includes list of ministers, with biographical notes. See also Presbyterians

Religious Records continued

Congregationalists

ANTROBUS, ALFRed. *History of the Wilts and East Somerset Congregational Union, prepared for the triple jubilee, 1797-1947.* Independent Press, 1947. Includes list of officers.

STRIBLING, S.B. *History of the Wilts and East Somerset Congregational Union, for the century after its commencement, 1797-1897, with some detailed account of the churches connected therewith.* [ ]: the Union, 1897. Includes notes on member churches, with many names.

'Congregational manse', *WFHS.* **40**, 1991, 11-13. Gives 42 names from a Swindon conveyance of 1868.

Independents

MAWBY, ROGER F. *Independent meeting to united church, 1740 to 1990: 250 years of Christian worship in Bradford-on-Avon.* [Bradford-on-Avon]: the author, 1990. Many names.

Hullavington

HURLEY, JOHN. 'Old records come to light", *W.F.H.S.* **28**, 1988, 23. List of members, 1827, and baptisms 1838-45, at Hullavington Independent Chapel.

Methodists

DREDGE, J. *The biographical record, or, sketches of the lives, experiences and happy deaths of members of the Wesleyan Society in the Salisbury Circuit.* The author, 1833.

CARTER, E.R. *History of Bath Road Methodist Church, 1880-1980.* Swindon: Stads, 1981. Includes list of ministers and many names.

Presbyterians

MURCH, JEROME. *A history of the Presbyterian and General Baptist churches in the West of England, with memoirs of some of their pastors.* R. Hunter, 1835. Includes lists of ministers in Gloucestershire, Wiltshire, Somerset, Dorset, Devon and Cornwall.

Quakers

PENNEY, NORMAN. 'Quakerism in Wiltshire", *W.N.Q.* **2**, 1896-8, 125-9, 163-83, 286-94, 342-5, 370-74, 426-32, 460-69, 518-24 & 566-71; **3**, 1899-1901, 16-20, 79-83, 119-23, 162-4, 228-31, 252-5, 317-20, 368-71, 423-6, 461-5, 511-14 & 546-9; **4**, 1902-4, 22-6, 63-5, 115-7, 160-63, 208-12, 257-63, 304-9, 371-4, 406-10, 452-5, 500-503 & 556-9; **5**, 1905-7, 17-21, 72-5, 117-9, 169-74, 223-6, 278-81, 304-7, 365-9, 403-6, 452-5, 514-7 & 549-52; **6**, 1908-10, 81-3, 130-34, 179-83, 224-31, 250-54, 305-8, 376-9, 412-4, 452-4 & 507-11; **7**, 1911-13, 6-9, 133-5, 179-81, 217-21, 270-71 & 512-6. See also **2**, 1896-8, 236-7; **3**, 1899-1901, 138-9. Includes notes on records, biographical notes on 'sufferers', marriages, births and burials, 17-19th c.

PENNEY, NORMAN. 'Wiltshire Quakers in America', *W.N.Q.* **4**, 1902-4, 139-40. See also **5**, 1905-7, 21-2.

FASSNIDGE, HAROLD. *The Quakers of Melksham, 1669-1950.* Bradford on Avon: Bradford on Avon Friends, 1992. Includes extensive list of trustees, 1698-1905, notes on meeting houses and burial grounds in Wiltshire, many biographical notes, pedigree of Lloyd, 18-20th c., etc.

Roman Catholics

WILLIAMS, J.A. *Catholic recusancy in Wiltshire 1660-1791.* Monograph series **1**. Catholic Record Society, 1968.

WILLIAMS, J.A. 'Wiltshire catholicism in the early 18th century: the diocesan returns of 1706', *Recusant history* **7**, 1963-4, 11-22. See also 146. Notes various mss. sources. General discussion.

OLIVER, GEORGE. *Collections illustrating the history of the Catholic religion in the counties of Cornwall, Devon, Dorset, Somerset, Wilts and Gloucester, in two parts, historical and biographical, with notices of the Dominican, Benedictine, & Franciscan orders in England.* C. Dolman, 1857.

'A list of Witlshire recusants', *W.N.Q.* **8**, 1914-16, 342-4. For works on Roman Catholic diocesan archives, see section 2B.

14. ESTATE AND FAMILY PAPERS

A. GENERAL

The records of estate administration (deeds, leases, surveys, accounts, etc.) are a rich mine of information for the genealogist. Many of these records have been published in full or part although far more still lie unexamined in the archives. For Wiltshire, a number of general collections of deeds have been published. The feet of fines (medieval deeds) are calendared in:

FRY, EDWARD ALEXANDER, ed. *A calendar of the feet of fines relating to the county of Wiltshire remaining in the Public Record Office, London, from their commencement in the reign of Richard I (1195) to the end of Henry III (1272).* Devizes: George Simpson & Co., for W.A.N.H.S., 1930.

PUGH, R.B., ed. *Abstracts of feet of fines relating to Wiltshire for the reigns of Edward I and Edward II.* W.R.S. 1, 1939.

ELRINGTON, C.R., ed. *Abstracts of feet of fines relating to Wiltshire for the reign of Edward III.* W.R.S. 29, 1974.

KIRBY, J.L., ed. *Abstracts of feet of fines relating to Wiltshire, 1377-1509.* W.R.S. 41, 1986.

FRY, E.A. 'A calendar of feet of fines for Wiltshire', *W.N.Q.* 2-8, 1896-1916, passim. Henry VII—Elizabeth I. Not completed.

Other published calendars, extracts, and notes on Wiltshire deeds in general include:

'The value of old parchment documents in genealogical research', *Topographical quarterly* 4(3), 1936, 282-8. Calendar of deeds collected by a bookseller.

PAFFORD, J.H.P., ed. 'Wiltshire deeds in Bath Public Library, 1437-60', in WILLIAMS, N.J., ed. *Collectanea.* W.R.S. 12, 1956, 168-75. From the Lacock area, 15th c.

CUNNINGTON, B.H. 'Some Wiltshire manorial documents', *W.A.M.* 49(175), 1941, 483. Brief list of documents in the W.A.N.H.S. library.

KIDSTON, GEORGE. 'The Society's mss: various documents presented by the British Record Society', *W.A.M.* 45(155), 1931, 459-69. Calendar of various 18th c. deeds, mainly relating to Bowood, the Neale family, Sherston, Stourton and Great Wishford, etc.

'Ancient Wiltshire deeds', *W.N.Q.* 8, 1914-16, 33-9 & 109-17. Medieval-17th c. deeds of various places.

Many other works relating to deeds are listed in the following sub-sections. Two other types of document must be mentioned here. The process of enclosing land from open field resulted in the creation of many documents. Enclosure awards usually include complete lists of owners and tenants; Wiltshire genealogists are fortunate that a full calendar of these documents has been published:

SANDELL, R.E., ed. *Abstracts of Wiltshire inclosure awards and agreements.* W.R.S. 25, 1971. This supersedes two previous works:

TATE, W.E. 'A hand list of Wiltshire enclosure acts and awards', *W.A.M.* 51(183), 1945, 127-73.

Calendar of enclosure awards deposited at the county record room at Devizes. Marlborough: Clerk of the Peace Office, 1900.

Of equal importance to the genealogist are the tithe apportionment awards of the mid-nineteenth century which also list owners and tenants:

SANDELL, R.E., ed. *Abstracts of Wiltshire tithe apportionments.* W.R.S. 30, 1975.

B. PRIVATE ESTATES

Many families have preserved deeds and papers relating to their estates and financial affairs. Some had interests covering wide areas of the county, and publications relating to these interests are listed here.

Baynton

FREEMAN, JANE, ed. *The commonplace book of Sir Edward Baynton of Bromham.* W.R.S. 43, 1988. Mainly concerns his family, estates, and political activity. 17th c.

Berkeley

JEAYES, ISAAC HERBERT. *Descriptive catalogue of the charters and muniments in the possession of Lord Fitzhardinge at Berkeley Castle.* Bristol: C.T. Jefferies & Sons, 1892. Calendar of charters, wills, accounts, manorial rolls, etc., relating to Wiltshire and Gloucestershire. Includes pedigree of Berkeley.

Bonham

'The Society's mss', *W.A.M.* 36(113), 1910, 439-47. Deeds relating to the Bonham and Westley families.

Broke

BLOOM, J. HARVEY, ed. *The cartae antiquae of Lord Willoughby de Broke, part IV: Wiltshire. Pulton, Bathampton, Codforde, Hanging Langford, West Harnam.* Hemsworth: C.E. Turner, [18—?]. Deed abstracts.

Estate and Family Papers continued

Clark
BECKINSALE, R.P., ed. *The Trowbridge woollen industry, as illustrated by the stock books of John and Thomas Clark, 1804-1824*. W.R.S. **6**, 1951. Transcript of accounts, giving many names.

Duchy of Lancaster
'Duchy of Lancaster: survey of its manors in Co.Wilts, taken 33 Eliz (A.D. 1591)', *W.A.M.* **6**(17), 1860, 186-200.

Gaby
COWARD, EDWARD. 'William Gaby, his booke 1656', *W.A.M.* **46**, 1932-3, 50-57 & 336-49. Common-place book, largely consisting of accounts, giving many names from the Netherstreet area.

Goddard
MABBS, A.W. *Documents relating to the Goddard family of North Wiltshire*. Typescript. Swindon: Central Library, 1960. Calendar of deeds and other family papers.

Herbert, Earls of Pembroke
HORWOOD, ALFRED J. 'The manuscripts of the Right Honourable the Earl of Pembroke at Wilton House', in HISTORICAL MANUSCRIPTS COMMISSION *Ninth report ..., part II*. C.3773-1. H.M.S.O., 1884, 379-84. Medieval deeds relating to Wilton Abbey, etc.
RUNDLE, PENELOPE. 'Wilton House records', *W.F.H.S.* **19**, 1985, 24-7. Description of the archives of the Herbert family.
KERRIDGE, ERIC, ed. *Surveys of the manors of Philip, first Earl of Pembroke and Montgomery, 1631-2*. W.R.S. **9**, 1953.

Hungerford
SANDELL, R. 'The Jackson papers', *W.A.M.* **57**(207), 1959, 263-4. Relating to the Hungerford family.
'The manuscripts of the Earl of Radnor, at Longford Castle, Salisbury', in HISTORICAL MANUSCRIPTS COMMISSION *Fifteenth report ... appendix; part X*. C.9472. H.M.S.O., 1899, 161-72. Relating to the Hungerford family, medieval-17th c.

Neale
NEALE, JOHN ALEXANDER. *Charters and records of Neales of Berkeley, Yate and Corsham*. Mackie & Co., 1906. See also supplements of 1927 and 1929. Mainly relating to Wiltshire and Gloucestershire.

Tropenall
DAVIES, J., ed. *The Tropenall cartulary: being the contents of an old Wiltshire muniment chest*. 2 vols. Devizes: Wiltshire Archaeological and Natural History Society, 1908. 15th c. cartulary of the Tropenall family of Corsham; includes pedigrees of Tropenall and Percy. Related works include:
DAVIES, J. SILVESTER. 'The Tropenall cartulary', *W.A.M.* **32**(97), 1902, 194-205.
'The Tropenall cartulary', *W.N.Q.* **6**, 1908-10, 89-96.
'Tropenall memoranda', *W.A.M.* **37**(118), 1912, 542-92.

Westley
See Bonham

Wyndham
PUGH, C.W. 'Some domestic and other bills of the Wyndham family (Salisbury)', *W.A.M.* **46**(158), 1933, 185-97. Gives names of many 18-19th c. tradesmen.

Many estate records relating to particular localities are in print, and are listed here by place:

Aldbourne
ELLIS, J.R. 'The Parliamentary enclosure of Aldbourne', *W.A.M.* **68B**, 1973, 89-108. Gives names of many landowners and occupiers, early 19th c.

Alderton
PAGE-TURNER, FREDK. A. 'Six deeds, etc., put into English, relating to Alderton, Co.Wilts ...', *W.N.Q.* **8**, 1914-16, 308-15. 14th c. deeds.

Alton Barnes
RICKARD, R.L., ed. *Progress notes of Warden Woodward for the Wiltshire estates of New College, Oxford, 1659-1675*. W.R.S. **13**, 1957. Includes court rolls, rentals, terriers, etc., relating to Alton Barnes, Colerne, and Stert.

Amesbury
HUGHES, G.W.G. 'Notes on the courts leet and baron in Amesbury, Wilts', *W.A.M.* **47**(165), 1936, 521-5. 18-19th c.

Amesbury Earls
PUGH, R.B., ed. *Calendar of Antrobus deeds before 1625*. W.R.S. **3**, 1947. Relating primarily to Amesbury Earls, Amesbury Priors, Dawbeneys, and Souths manors, etc.

Amesbury Priors
See Amesbury Earls

Estate and Family Papers continued

Beckington
See Bradford on Avon

Braden Forest
MANLEY, F.H. 'Parliamentary surveys of the crown land in Braden Forest (1651)', *W.A.M.* **46**(158), 1933, 176-84.

Bradford on Avon
LINDEGAARD, PATRICIA. 'Manorial court records', *W.F.H.S.* **27**, 1987, 34. Brief note concerning Bradford on Avon court rolls, including list of some names mentioned 1791-1801.
KNUBLEY, E.P. 'The Society's mss: abstracts of deeds relating to the family of Methuen at Bradford, Corsham, Melksham, Chitterne and Beckington', *W.A.M.* **43**(145), 1926, 401-31. Calendar, 17-19th c.
STOTE, A.W. 'The Society's mss: abstracts of copies of court rolls and other documents relating to the manors of Bradford & Westwood', *W.A.M.* **41**(134), 1921, 217-63.

Bremhill
See Calstone

Brixton Deverill
PIERREPONT, J.R. 'The manor of Brixton Deverill: a custumal and an extent of the thirteenth century', *W.A.M.* **78**, 1984, 55-61. Includes names.

Broad Hinton
STORY-MASKELYNE, A.ST.J. 'Two surveys of the manour of Broad Hinton 1708/9 and 1751', *W.A.M.* **39**(125), 1916, 382-91.

Broad Town
GODDARD, E.H. 'A terrier of the common fields belonging to Broad Town & Thornhill in the county of Wilts. 1725', *W.A.M.* **46**(159), 1933, 366-79.

Bromham
REYNOLDS, SUSAN, ed. 'Pleas in the Liberty of the abbot of Battle at Bromham 1289', in WILLIAMS, N.J., ed. *Collectanea*. W.R.S. **12**, 1956, 129-41.

Bupton
See Cliffe Pypard

Calstone
KERRY, EARL OF. 'The customs of the manors of Calstone and Bremhill', *W.A.M.* **43**(143), 1925, 192-206. 1621 customary, giving many names of tenants.

Castle Combe
SCROPE, G. POULETT. *History of the manor and ancient barony of Castle Combe, in the county of Wilts., chiefly compiled from original mss. and chartularies at Castle Combe, with memoirs of the families of Dunstanville, Badlesmere, Tiptoft, Scrope, Fastolf, etc.* J.W. Nichols & Son, 1852. Includes rental, 1340, extent, 1454, extracts from court rolls and accounts, etc.

Charlton
See Lacock

Chitterne
See Bradford on Avon

Cliffe Pypard
'The Society's mss: Clyffe Pypard, Bupton', *W.A.M.* **35**(109), 1908, 460-96. Includes calendar of 56 deeds, 13-17th c.

Cholderton
'Records of Cholderton', *W.N.Q.* **1**, 1893-5, 500-6 & 550-5; **2**, 1896-8, 7-17, 68-75, 104-11 & 155-62. Abstracts of medieval deeds, etc.
'Cholderton: [additional records]', *W.N.Q.* **4**, 1902-4, 552-6. Deeds 13-17th c.

Colerne
See Alton Barnes

Corsham
See Bradford on Avon

Corton
'Survey, temp Phil. & Mar., of various estates late belonging to the Earl of Devon', *Topographer & genealogist* **1**, 1846, 43-58, 145-53, 223-8 & 343-8. Includes survey of an estate at Corton, Wiltshire.

Cote
See Lacock

Dawbeneys
See Amesbury Earls

Durrington
KIRBY, T.F. 'Records of the manor of Durrington, Wilts', *Archaeologia* **59**, 1904, 75-82. Medieval deeds, etc.

Great Somerford
See Seagry

Grittleton
MANLEY, F.H. 'The Society's mss: Grittleton deeds', *W.A.M.* **44**(149), 1928, 215-35. Abstracts of 74 deeds.

Estate and Family Papers continued

Grittleton continued

SHICKLE, C.W., & MANLEY, F.H. 'The Society's mss: Grittleton manor rolls, 1613-25, 1627-47', *W.A.M.* **44**(151), 1929, 429-73.

Hannington

FRY, C.B. *Hannington: the records of a Wiltshire parish*. Gloucester: John Bellows, 1935. The author was lord of the manor, and the book includes many extracts from manorial records and deeds, as well as a list of clergy, etc.

Highworth Hundred

See Sevenhampton

Lacock

HINTON, F.H. 'Notes on the court books of the manors of Lacock, Charlton, Liddington with Cote, and Nethermore (chiefly 1583 to 1603)', *W.A.M.* **50**(188), 1944, 459-78. General discussion.

Liddington

See Lacock

Market Lavington

KITE, EDWARD. 'Some notes on the Delamere family and their chantry at Market Lavington', *W.N.Q.* **3**, 1899-1901, 410-20 & 465-70. 13-15th c., includes survey of the chantry lands, naming tenants, mid-16th c., also a list of chaplains.

Melksham

See Bradford on Avon

Salisbury

NEVILL, EDMUND. 'Salisbury in 1455 (Liber Niger)', *W.A.M.* **37**(115), 1911, 66-91. Lists tenants of the Bishop of Salisbury.

MALDEN, A.R. 'Survey of the Close in 1649: transcript of a ms. in the Diocesan Registry, Salisbury', *Transactions of the Salisbury Field Club* **1**, 1890-91, 95-9, 132-8 & 167-71; **2**, 1892-6, 81-7.

Seagry

MANLEY, F.H. 'The Society's mss: the deeds of Seagry House', *W.A.M.* **43**(144), 1926, 285-310. Deeds relate to Seagry and Great Somerford, 16-18th c.

Sevenhampton

FARR, M.W., ed. *Accounts and surveys of the Wiltshire lands of Adam de Stratton*. W.R.S. **14**, 1959. Relate to 13th c. Sevenhampton.

Sevenhampton continued

PUGH, RALPH B., ed. *Court rolls of the Wiltshire manors of Adam de Stratton*. W.R.S. **24**, 1970. Relating to Sevenhampton, Highworth Hundred, and Stratton St.Margaret; 13th c.

Sherston Magna

SYMONDS, W. 'Five ancient deeds at Sherston Magna', *W.N.Q.* **6**, 1908-10, 399-404 & 447-52. 15-16th c., includes will of Johanna Baker, 1404.

SYMONDS, W. 'Sherston manor rolls', *W.N.Q.* **7**, 1911-13, 173-9, 245-51, 298-303, 370-3, 403-6, 486-92 & 536-40; **8**, 1914-16, 17-20 & 88-93. Transcript of 17th c. rolls. Sherston Magna.

Souths

See Amesbury Earls

Stert

See Alton Barnes

Stratton St.Margaret

See Sevenhampton

Thornhill

See Broad Town

Vasterne

See Wootton Bassett

Wanborough

[PHILLIPPS, THOMAS, ed.] *Wanborough court rolls, 1649*. [Middle Hill]: [the editor, 184-?]. Includes parochial assessment, 1701.

West Kington

STOATE, T.L., ed. *A survey of West County manors, 1525: the lands of Cecily, Marchioness of Dorset, Lady Harington and Bonville, in Cornwall, Devon, Dorset, Somerset and Wiltshire*. Bristol: the editor, 1979. Includes West Kington.

Westwood

See Bradford on Avon

Wilsford

DUKE, R.E.H. 'Wilsford rent roll, 1499', *W.N.Q.* **8**, 1914-16, 351-7 & 398-401.

Wootton Bassett

GOUGH, W., ed. 'Documents in the Society's library concerning Wootton Bassett and Vasterne', *W.A.M.* **49**(174), 1941, 313-30. Rentals of Wootton Bassett, 1674, and of Vasterne, 1666, etc.

GOUGH, W. 'The Society's mss: abstracts of deeds, &c., of Little Park, Wootton Bassett', *W.A.M.* **44**(147), 1927, 30-40. Abstracts of 40 deeds, etc.

Estate and Family Papers continued

C. ECCLESIASTICAL ESTATES AND CHARTULARIES

In the medieval period, a great deal of landed property was owned by ecclesiastical institutions such as churches, dioceses, monasteries, etc. Ecclesiastical estate records have survived much better than those of private families, and many are in print. An early survey of church lands in Wiltshire is printed in:

POWELL, W. RAYMOND, ed. 'Two royal surveys of church lands in Wiltshire during the Interdict', in *Interdict documents*. Pipe Roll Society **72** (N.S. **34**), 1958 (1960), 3-32. Constitutes an early directory of the principal villagers of 25% of Wiltshire parishes, listing 300 names.

Much land was lost by the church at the reformation—but much remained. Terriers identify the lands held by particular churches; those for Wiltshire are listed in:

HOLGATE, C.W. 'Wiltshire parochial terriers', *Salisbury Diocesan gazette* **12**, 1899, 168-70.

Surviving cartularies, i.e., books of deeds, for Wiltshire monasteries are listed in:

K[ITE], E. 'The cartularies of Wiltshire abbeys and monasteries', *W.N.Q.* **4**, 1902-4, 229-30. See also 330-31 and **5**, 1905-7, 233-6. Printed cartularies and other estate records of Wiltshire ecclesiastical institutions are listed here by institution:

Bradenstoke Priory

LONDON, VERA C.M., ed. *The cartulary of Bradenstoke Priory*. W.R.S. **35**, 1979.

Edington

STEVENSON, JANET H., ed. *The Edington cartulary*. W.R.S. **42**, 1987.

Lacock Abbey

ROGERS, KENNETH H., ed. *Lacock Abbey charters*. W.R.S. **34**, 1979.

BOWLES, W.L., AND NICHOLS, JOHN GOUGH. *Annals and antiquities of Lacock Abbey in the county of Wilts, with memorials of the foundress, Ela, Countess of Salisbury, and of the Earls of Salisbury, of the houses of Sarisbury and Longespe, including notices of the monasteries of Bradenstoke, Hinton, and Farley*. John Bowyer Nichols and Son, 1835. Includes abstract of chartulary.

Lacock Abbey continued

CLARK-MAXWELL, W.G. 'The customs of four manors of the Abbey of Lacock', *W.A.M.* **32**(98), 1902, 311-46. Medieval; manors of Bishopstrow, Heddington, Hatherop and Lacock. Many names.

CLARK-MAXWELL, W.G. 'The earliest charters of the Abbey of Lacock', *W.A.M.* **35**(108), 1907, 191-209.

Malmesbury Abbey

BREWER, J.S., AND MARTIN, CHARLES TRICE., eds. *Registrum Malmesburiense: the register of Malmesbury Abbey* ... 2 vols. Rolls series **72**. H.M.S.O., 1879-80. Includes medieval rent rolls, which are also printed in *Archaeologia* **37**, 1857, 273-303.

Salisbury. St.Nicholas Hospital

WORDSWORTH, CHR., ed. *The fifteenth century chartulary of St.Nicholas Hospital, Salisbury, with other records*. Wiltshire Record Society publications **3**. Salisbury: Brown & Co., 1902.

A number of institutions in other counties held property in Wiltshire. See:

Glastonbury Abbey

WATKIN, AELRED, ed. *The great chartulary of Glastonbury, vol.III*. Somerset Record Society **64**, 1956. This volume calendars deeds relating to the abbey's lands in Wiltshire and various other counties. For other works relating to Glastonbury lands, see *Somerset: a genealogical bibliography*.

Lewes

BUDGEN, W., AND SALZMAN, L.F., eds. *The Wiltshire, Devonshire and Dorsetshire portion of the Lewes chartulary, with London and Essex documents from the Surrey portion*. [ ]: Sussex Record Society, 1943.

Windsor Castle. St.George's Chapel

DALTON, JOHN NEALE, ed. *The manuscripts of St.George's Chapel, Windsor Castle*. Windsor: The Dean & Canons, 1957. These relate to property in 18 Wiltshire parishes, as well as to estates in many other counties.

D. MANORIAL DESCENTS, etc.

From deeds and other estate records, it is usually possible to trace the descent of manors and other lands. A number of descents have been published, and are listed here by place:

Estate and Family Papers continued

Amesbury

PUGH, R.B. 'The early history of the manors of Amesbury', *W.A.M.* **52**(187), 1947, 70-110. Traces descent.

Avebury

'Notes on Wiltshire parishes: Avebury', *W.N.Q.* **8**, 1914-16, 214-24, 270-77. Traces descent of the manor.

Axford

FRY, E.A. 'Manor of Axford, Co.Wilts', *W.N.Q.* **7**, 1911-13, 265-9. Medieval descent of manor.

Bradford on Avon. Kingston House

JACKSON, J.E. 'Kingston House, Bradford', *W.A.M.* **1**(3), 1854, 265-302. Hall and Pierrepoint families; includes pedigrees, 15-19th c., and calendar of 97 deeds.

Bromham. Nonsuch House

'Nonsuch House, Bromham', *W.N.Q.* **2**, 1896-8, 190-201. Descent through Baynton and Norris, 17-19th c.

Castle Combe

SCROPE, G. POULETT. 'History of the Wiltshire manors subordinate to the barony of Castle Combe', *W.A.M.* **2**(5), 1855, 261-89. Medieval descents.

Chalfield Magna

WALKER, THOMAS LARKINS. *The history and antiquities of the manor house and church of Great Chalfield, Wiltshire* ... The author, 1837. Includes descent of the manor, medieval-17th c., and list of clergy and patrons.

Draycot Cerne

LONG, CHARLES EDWARD. 'Descent of the manor of Draycot Cerne, with pedigree of Cerne and Heryng', *W.A.M.* **3**(8), 1857, 178-81. Medieval.

East Winterslow

COX, TREVOR. 'The manor of East Winterslow', *W.A.M.* **50**(180), 1944, 379-81. Descent of manor, 12-20th c.
COX, H.B. TREVOR. 'Manor of East Winterslow (part III)', *W.A.M.* **51**(184), 1946, 264-6. Traces medieval descent of Roche Old Court.

Erlestoke

WATSON-TAYLOR, JOHN. 'Erlestoke and its manor lords', *W.A.M.* **33**, 1904, 295-311 & 377-83; **34**, 1906, 42-102. Includes medieval pedigrees of Mandeville and Fitzherbert.

Hazelbury

KIDSTON, G.J. *A history of the manor of Hazelbury, with some account of the families of Croke, Bonham, Yound of Bristol, Speke and Tempest.* Methuen, 1936. Includes descent of the manor, with pedigrees.

Lacock

CHETTLE, H.F. 'Lacock Abbey', *W.A.M.* **51**(182), 1945, 1-13. Includes descent since the Reformation.

Longleat

JACKSON, J.E. 'The history of Longleat', *W.A.M.* **3**(9), 1857, 281-312. Descent of the property.

Malmesbury. Burton Hill House

MANLEY, F.H. 'Burton Hill House and its owners', *W.N.Q.* **8**, 1914-16, 433-9. Malmesbury. Traces descent.

Melksham. Place House

KITE, EDWARD. 'Place House, Melksham and its owners', *W.N.Q.* **4**, 1902-4, 241-52, 337-49 & 433-40. Includes pedigrees (one folded) of Brouncker, 16-17th c., and Selfe, 17-18th c., with Selfe wills.

Monkton Farleigh

JACKSON, J.E. 'The history of the Priory, of Monkton Farley', *W.A.M.* **4**(12), 1858, 267-84. Includes post-Reformation descent.

Old Lackham House

'Old Lackham House and its owners', *W.N.Q.* **3**, 1899-1901, 1-6, 49-62, 167-74. Not completed.

Salisbury. Church House

EVERETT, C.R. 'Notes on the history of the Diocesan Church House, Salisbury', *W.A.M.* **49**(175), 1941, 435-79. Includes folded pedigrees of Coke, Stone, Webb, Newman, and Chafyn.

Salisbury. The Close

EDWARDS, KATHLEEN. 'The houses of Salisbury Close in the fourteenth century', *Journal of the British Archaeological Association* 3rd series **4**, 1939, 55-115. Includes extensive lists of clergy occupants of houses in the Close.
EVERETT, C.R. 'Notes on the decanal and other houses in the Close of Sarum', *W.A.M.* **50**(181), 1944, 425-45. Traces occupants.
ROBERTSON, DORA H. 'A history of no.11, The Close, Salisbury', *W.A.M.* **52**(189), 1948, 307-17. Traces descent.

Estate and Family Papers continued

Salisbury. Minster Street

REEVES, J.A., & BONNEY, H.M. 'No.15, Minster Street, Salisbury: a fourteenth century timber framed house', *W.A.M.* **76**, 1981, 99-104. Includes 14-15th c. descent.

Sheldon

G[IBBS], E. *Sheldon Manor.* St.Ives: Beric Tempest & Co., 1982. Traces descent of the manor.

Southwick Court

KITE, ed. 'Southwick Court and its owners', *W.N.Q.* **1**, 1893-5, 556-60; **2**, 1896-8, 24-9. Descent through Greyville, Stafford, Cheney, Willoughby, Bush, Bayley, Long, etc.

Stockton

NIGHTINGALE, J.E. 'The descent of the manor of Stockton', *W.A.M.* **24**(24), 1889, 281-6. Medieval.

M., A.S. 'The descent of the manor of Stockton', *W.A.M.* **26**(77), 1892, 270-77. 16-17th c., mainly concerned with Toppe family.

Urchfont

POLLOCK, H. RIVERS. 'Notes on Erchfont manor house', *W.A.M.* **46**(157), 1932, 35-49. Includes notes on occupants from 17th c., especially Pynsert, Compton and Salmon families.

Wardour Castle

PUGH, R.B. *Old Wardour Castle, Wiltshire.* H.M.S.O., 1988. Includes brief descent of the castle, medieval-20th c.

15. NATIONAL, COUNTY AND LOCAL ADMINISTRATION

A. *NATIONAL AND COUNTY*

Official lists of names, such as tax lists and census records, have already been dealt with. There are, however, many other records of central and local administration which can yield useful information to the genealogist. At the county level, Quarter Sessions was the most important arm of government until the 19th century. For Quarter Sessions archives, consult section 2B above. A number of works provide extracts:

MERRIMAN, R.W. 'Extracts from the records of the Wiltshire quarter session', *W.A.M.* **20**(60), 1882, 322-41, **21**(61), 1884, 75-120; **22**(64), 1885, 1-38; **22**(65), 1885, 212-31. General discussion.

JOHNSON, H.C., ed. *Wiltshire county records: minutes of proceedings in sessions, 1563 and 1574 to 1592.* W.R.S. **4**. 1949.

CUNNINGTON, B. HOWARD, ed. *Records of the county of Wilts: being extracts from the quarter sessions great rolls of the seventeenth century.* Devizes: George Simpson & Co., 1932.

CUNNINGTON, B. HOWARD. *Presentments of the Grand Jury of the Quarter Sessions etc. held at Marlborough, 1706 to 1751, and some 18th and early 19th century inquests.* Devizes: George Simpson & Co., 1929.

FOWLE, J.P.M., ed. *Wiltshire quarter sessions and assizes, 1736.* W.R.S. **11**. 1955.

Most of Wiltshire's leading families have sent a member to represent the county or a local borough in the House of Commons. Wiltshire members of parliament are listed in:

MANLEY, F.H. 'A list of the representatives in Parliament from 1295-1832 for the county and burroughs of Wiltshire as given in the Parliamentary return of 1872', *W.A.M.* **47**(158), 1935, 177-264.

See also:

CROUCH, W.B. *Parliamentary history*, in THOMSON, T.R., ed. *Materials for a history of Cricklade* **6**. Oxford: Oxford U.P., for Cricklade Historical Society, 1961. Brief biographies of M.P.'s.

'Members of Parliament for Ludgershall', *W.A.M.* **34**(104), 1905, 151-6.

For many centuries, the sheriff was the leading officer in the county. Their names are listed chronologically in:

JACKSON, J.E. 'Sheriffs of Wiltshire', *W.A.M.* **3**(8), 1857, 189-235, and **18**(52), 1879, 7-8.

Administration *continued*

National and county administration has produced a wide range of documents of interest to genealogists. A few of these have been published and are listed here chronologically:

PHILLIPPS, THOMAS, ed. *Wiltshire pipe rolls, temp. Henrici II, A.D. 1159 ad 1179.* Middle Hill Press, 1853.

MAITLAND, F.W. *Three rolls of the king's court in the reign of Richard the First, 1194-1195.* Publications of the Pipe Roll Society **14**, 1891. Includes one Wiltshire roll.

'A feodary of lands in Wiltshire', *W.N.Q.* **8**, 1914-16, 328-31, 410-14 & 514-8. List of knights fees, 13th c.

CHALLENGER, SHEILA, ed. 'Accounts for works on the royal mills and castle at Marlborough, 1237-8 and 1238-9', in WILLIAMS, N.J., ed. *Collectanea.* W.R.S. **12**, 1956, 1-49. Gives many names.

MEEKINGS, C.A.F., ed. *Crown pleas of the Wiltshire Eyre, 1249.* W.R.S. **16**, 1961.

CLANCHY, M.T., ed. *Civil pleas of the Wiltshire Eyre, 1249.* W.R.S. **26**, 1971.

MAITLAND, F.W., ed. *Select please in manorial and other seignorial courts, vol.I: reigns of Henry III and Edward I.* Selden Society publications **2**, 1889. Includes pleas of Whorwelsdown Hundred, 1262, with many names.

PUGH, RALPH B., ed. *Wiltshire gaol delivery and trailbaston trials, 1275-1306.* W.R.S. **33**, 1978.

FARR, BRENDA, ed. *The rolls of Highworth Hundred, 1275-1287.* 2 vols. W.R.S. **21-2**, 1966-8.

LATHAM, R.E., & MEEKINGS, C.A.F., eds. *The veredictum of Chippenham Hundred, 1281.* in WILLIAMS, N.J., ed. *Collectanea.* W.R.S. **12**, 1956, 50-128. From the Eyre court.

CONYERS, ANGELA, ed. *Wiltshire extents for debts, Edward I-Elizabeth I.* W.R.S. **28**, 1973.

PELHAM, R.A. 'The provisioning of Edward I's journey through Wiltshire in 1302', *W.A.M.* **54**(196), 1952, 350-60. Accounts, giving names of suppliers.

JONES, W.H. 'The nomina villarum for Wiltshire', *W.A.M.* **12**(34), 1870, 1-43. Lists lords of hundreds, boroughs and manors, etc. 1316.

THOMPSON, E.M. 'Offenders against the Statute of Labourers in Wiltshire, A.D. 1349', *W.A.M.* **33**(102), 1904, 385-409. From the Assize rolls, giving many names of labourers, etc.

JACKSON, J.E. 'The sheriff's turn, Co.Wilts, A.D. 1439', *W.A.M.* **13**(38), 1872. Court roll; many names.

CONDON, M.M., ed. 'A Wiltshire sheriff's notebook, 1464-5', in HUNNISETT, R.F., & POST, J.B. *Medieval legal records: in memory of C.A.F. Meekings.* H.M.S.O., 1978, 410-28.

MONEY, WALTER. 'The names of the nobility, gentry, and others in the County of Wilts who contributed to the defence of the county at the time of the Spanish armada invasion, in 1588', *W.A.M.* **23**(67), 1887, 31-33.

JACKSON, J.E. 'Longleat papers, A.D. 1553-1588', *W.A.M.* **14**, 1874, 192-216 & 237-52; **18**, 1879, 9-48 & 257-85; **19**, 1881, 254-66. Includes list of contributors to loan of 1571, list of freeholders, 1607-8, and various other papers relating to county government.

'Wiltshire tithe cases', *W.N.Q.* **1**, 1893-5, 454-8 & 538-42; **2**, 1896-8, 60-65. Extracts from various 17th c. cases.

MURPHY, W.P.D., ed. *The Earl of Hertford's lieutenancy papers, 1603-1612.* W.R.S. **23**, 1969. Mainly letters, but includes many names.

FRY, E.A. 'Knighthood compositions for Wiltshire', *W.N.Q.* **1**, 1893-5, 50-54 & 106-9. List of those fined for failing to attend Charles I's coronation to receive knighthoods.

COCKBURN, J.S., ed. *Western circuit assize orders, 1629-1648: a calendar.* Camden 4th series **17**. Royal Historical Society, 1976.

WAYLEN, J. 'The Falstone day-book', *W.A.M.* **26**(78), 1892, 343-91. Minute book of the Parliamentary County Committee, which met at Falstone, 1645-53; gives many names, with some biographical information.

PAFFORD, J.H.P., ed. *Accounts of the Parliamentary garrison of Great Chalfield and Malmesbury, 1645-1646.* W.R.S. **2**, 1940 (reprinted 1966).

CARRINGTON, F.A. 'Composition for estates in Wilts', *W.A.M.* **4**(11), 1858, 148-57. Includes list of royalists fined by Parliament for their 'delinquency' mid-17th c.

WAYLEN, JAMES. 'The Wiltshire compounders', *W.A.M.* **23**(69), 1887, 314-46; **24**, 1889, 58-103 & 308-44. Includes biographical notes on royalist 'compounders'.

RAVENHILL, W.W. 'Records of the rising in the West: John Penruddock, Hugh Grove, et socii, A.D. 1655', *W.A.M.* **13**, 1872, 119-88 & 252-73; **14**, 1874, 38-67; **15**, 1876, 1-41 & 235-6. Includes lists of prisoners, etc.

KEMPSON, E.G.H. 'Indictments for the coining of tokens in seventeenth-century Wiltshire', *British Numismatic Journal* **43**, 1973, 126-31. Gives names of men accused of illegal coining in the 1670s.

Administration continued

COLE, JEAN. 'More about the Monmouth rebellion, 1685', *W.F.H.S.* **33**, 1989, 10-12. Gives many names of rebels, from Wiltshire quarter sessions rolls, 1685-6.

MATCHAM, GEORGE. 'Wiltshire nonjurors, &c.', *W.A.M.* **16**(48), 1876, 337-8. List of those refusing the oath of allegiance to George I, 1715.

CRITTALL, ELIZABETH, ed. *The justicing notebook of William Hunt, 1744-1749.* W.R.S. **37**, 1982.

HUNNISETT, R.F., ed. *Wiltshire coroner's bills, 1752-1796.* W.R.S. **36**, 1981.

BARNES, TONY. 'Persons eligible to serve as jurymen, 1771', *W.F.H.S.* **14**, 1983, 11-15. In the Highworth area. List.

CHARITY COMMISSION. *Return comprising the reports made to the Charity Commissioners in the result of an inquiry held in every parish ... within ... Wilts into endowments, subject to the Charitable Trusts Act, 1853 to 1894, together with the reports ... concerning charities, 1818 to 1837.* 2 vols. H.M.S.O., 1901. Includes many notes on deeds, wills, trustees, etc.

THURSTON, E.J. *The magistrates of England and Wales: Western Circuit, Cornwall, Devonshire, Dorsetshire, Hampshire, Somersetshire, Wiltshire.* Hereford: Jakemans, 1940. Who's who style of listing.

B. *LOCAL ADMINISTRATION, etc.*

The records of parochial and borough administration—the accounts of overseers, churchwardens and other officers, settlement papers, rate lists, deeds, etc.—contain much information of genealogical value. They frequently provide the names, if nothing else, of the humble mass of the poor, who otherwise went unrecorded. Slack's *Poverty in early Stuart Salisbury*, listed below, is particularly useful in this regard as it lists many poor migrants to Salisbury from throughout Wiltshire and the adjacent counties.

Also included here are a number of works which include extracts from a wide range of records relating to particular parishes—deeds, monumental inscriptions, churchwardens' accounts, subsidies, court rolls, etc. Wiltshire borough and parochial records are listed in three works:

RATHBONE, MAURICE G., ed. *List of Wiltshire borough records earlier in date than 1836.* W.R.S. **5**, 1951.

GARDINER, CANON. *Rural deanery of Avebury (Cannings portion): inventories, terriers, memorial tablets, etc., church plate and bells, A.D. 1910.* [Avebury: Canon Gardiner, c.1918]. Includes list of documents in parish chests, and monumental inscriptions, together with much information on parochial administration in the early part of this century.

JACOBS, C.J. 'A brief catalogue of the contents of parish chests in the Devizes area', *W.A.M.* **53**(193), 1950, 447-57.

See also Carter's *Location of documents for Wiltshire parishes* listed in section 2B.

For settlement examination relating to Wiltshire migrants in Surrey, see:

COLE, JEAN A. 'Some Wiltshire settlement examinations found in Surrey records', *W.F.H.S.* **20**, 1986, 20-21.

Full details of nine Wiltshire migrants in Westleigh, Gloucestershire, are given in:

SHORT, GERALDINE. 'Westerleigh poor law records: strays from the settlement examinations in the records of the parish of Westleigh, Gloucestershire, north of Bristol', *W.F.H.S.* **32**, 1989, 32-3.

Wiltshire members of a 16th c. Ludlow, Shropshire, guild are listed in:

KEMPSON, E.G.H. 'A Shropshire guild at work in Wiltshire', *W.A.M.* **57**(206), 1958, 50-55.

Works relating to particular Wiltshire parishes include:

Box

MELLOR, A. SHAW. 'Box parish records: sidelights on life in a Wiltshire village in the past', *W.A.M.* **47**(164), 1936, 345-57. Includes list of documents in the parish chest, with extracts from them, including names.

MELLOR, A. SHAW. 'Extracts from the accounts of the overseers of the parish of Box, Wilts, from November 26th, 1727, to April 17th, 1748', *W.A.M.* **45**(154), 1931, 342-9. Includes list of paupers who were given 'apparell' in 1729.

Bradford on Avon

HEMBRY, PHYLLIS, ed. *Calendar of Bradford-on-Avon settlement examinations and removal orders, 1725-98.* W.R.S. **46**, 1990.

An account of the parochial charities of Bradford-on-Avon, Wilts. Bradford-on-Avon: J. Rawling, 1858.

Administration *continued*

Bratton
THOMPSON, E.M. 'Records of Wiltshire parishes: Bratton', *W.N.Q.* **2**, 1896-8, 271-9, 313-23, 357-68, 408-16, 452-60, 500-8 & 553-61; **3**, 1899-1901, 6-15, 69-78, 105-14, 154-61, 202-14, 242-52, 306-17, 346-54, 404-10, 448-54, 496-505 & 525-33; **4**, 1902-4, 5-11, 53-60, 107-15, 202-8 & 253-6. Deeds, inquisitions post mortem, lay subsidies, wills, etc. Medieval-19th c.

Broad Town
BRADFORD, JAMES E.G. *Some particulars relating to a charity called the Broad Town Charity, in the county of Wilts, founded by Her Grace Sarah, Duchess Dowager of Somerset, deceased, for apprenticing poor male children* ... Swindon: R. Astill, 1882. Lists many trustees.

Calne
EVERETT, C.R., ed. 'A rate made this 19th day of August anno dom. 1695, for & towards the repair of the p.ish church of Calne, etc., being two poor rates', *W.A.M.* **47**(164), 1936, 340-4.
MABBS, A.W., ed. *Guild steward's book of the borough of Calne, 1561-1688.* W.R.S. **7**, 1953.

Chippenham
GOLDNEY, FREDERICK HASTINGS. *Records of Chippenham relating to the borough, from its incorporation by Queen Mary, 1554, to its reconstruction by Act of Parliament, 1889, comprising extracts from the minute books and registers of accounts of the corporation, together with copies and references from the charters, deeds and documents in the Borough chest.* Diprose, Bateman & Co., 1889. Includes pedigree of Goldney, 16-19th c.
HINTON, F.H. 'Notes on the records and accounts of the overseers of the poor of Chippenham, 1691-1805', *W.A.M.* **46**(159), 1933, 312-35. General discussion, not a transcript, but gives some names.
See also Langley

Chippenham Union
PHILPOTT, JEAN. 'Records of the Union workhouse', *W.F.H.S.* **14**, 1984, 22-4. General discussion of the records of Chippenham Union, 19th c., with a few names.

Chisledon
'The Society's ms: Chisledon and Draycot', *W.A.M.* **30**, 1899, 38-54, 126-42 & 307-33; **31**, 1901, 49-68 & 135-96. Includes various pedigrees, Chisledon poor rate, 1649, poll tax, 1666, land tax, 1733, 1738 and 1780, and many other deeds and documents.

Devizes
CUNNINGTON, B. HOWARD. *Some annals of the borough of Devizes: being a series of extracts from the corporation records* ... 2 vols. Devizes: George Simpson & Co., 1925-6. Covers 1555-1835.
KITE, EDWARD. 'The churches of Devizes', *W.A.M.* **2**, 1855, 213-56 & 302-32. Includes monumental inscriptions, notes on the Coventry family, 14-15th c., calendar of 28 deeds, extracts from churchwardens accounts, list of rectors and chaplains, folded pedigree of Garth, 16-19th c., etc.

Draycot
See Chisledon

Grittleton
JACKSON, J.E. *The history of the parish of Grittleton, in the county of Wilts.* J.B. Nichols & Son for the Wiltshire Topographical Society, 1843. Includes pedigrees of White, Houlton, and Greene, list of rectors, monumental inscriptions, etc.

Heytesbury
HAMMOND, J.J. 'Heytesbury almshouse accounts, 1592', *W.A.M.* **44**(149), 1928, 257-9.

Hilmarton
GODDARD, CANON. 'Copy of the terrier of the parish of Hilmarton, Wilts, dated January 17th, 1704', *W.A.M.* **24**(71), 1889, 125-6. Names some landowners and occupiers.

Lacock
HINTON, F.H. 'Notes on the administration of the relief of the poor of Lacock', *W.A.M.* **49**(173), 1940, 166-218. General discussion, with some names.

Langley
'Quarrel between the inhabitants of the village of Langley and the town of Chippenham', *W.N.Q.* **2**, 1896-8, 470-73. Includes list of 32 men killed or wounded in a fight, 1822.

Latton
TOWNSEND, JOHN. 'The churchwardens of Latton, 1676-1895', *W.F.H.S.* **30**, 1988, 32-3. General discussion.

Administration continued

Little Somerford
'Maudit's Park tithe dispute', *W.N.Q.* **8**, 1914-16, 125-31. Dispute concerning farm at Little Somerford, 1697, giving many names.

Malmesbury
LUCE, SIR RICHARD H. 'An old Malmesbury minute book', *W.A.M.* **47**(164), 1936, 321-9. Description of 17-18th c. minute book.

T., B.C. 'Catalogue of the high stewards of the borough of Malmesbury, Wilts', *Collectanea topographica et genealogica* **6**, 1840, 297-8. 17-18th c.

CUNNINGHAM, T.S., & THOMPSON, E.M. 'Records of Marden', *W.N.Q.* **7**, 388-96, 465-9, 519-22 & 559-64; **8**, 1914-16, 7-11, 58-61, 118-24, 155-62, 206-12 & 251-61. Medieval deeds, 16-17th c. subsidies, inquisitions post mortem, legal proceedings, tithe valuation, 1807, etc.

Market Lavington
PLEYDELL-BOUVERIE, E.O. 'A burial incident at Market Lavington, and a remarkable parochial agreement of the eighteenth century', *W.A.M.* **35**(109), 1908, 445-59. Agreement includes the names of landowners and occupiers, 1742.

Marlborough
CUNNINGTON, B. HOWARD, ed. *The orders, decrees and ordinances of the borough and town of Marlborough (Wilts)* ... Devizes: George Simpson & Co., 1929. Includes a few 17-18th c. names.

Mere
BAKER, T.H., ed. 'The churchwardens' accounts of Mere', *W.A.M.* **35**(107), 1907, 23-92 and 210-82. Transcript, 16-17th c.

BAKER, T.H. 'Mere churchwardens' book', *W.N.Q.* **2**, 1896-8, 484-5. Extracts, 18th c.

'Mere churchwardens' accounts', *Notes & queries for Somerset & Dorset* **2**, 1891, 314-7.

'The names of such inhabitants of the town and pish of Mere aforesaid as have contributed towards the redemption of many poor christians lately taken by the Turkish pirates ... 1670', *W.A.M.* **49**(174), 1941, 355-6. Lists many names.

North Newnton
KITE, ed. 'Notes on the churchwardens' accounts of the parish of North Newnton, Wilts', *W.N.Q.* **6**, 1908-10, 261-6. 16th c.

Romsey
STAGG, STELLA. 'Orders of removal—parish certificates, etc.: Romsey/Wiltshire', *W.F.H.S.* **28**, 1988, 27. Lists names.

Salisbury
SLACK, PAUL, ed. *Poverty in early Stuart Salisbury*. W.R.S. **31**. 1975. Includes register of passports for vagrants, 1598-1669, and various surveys—effectively censuses—of the poor.

'Muniments of the Corporation of Salisbury', in HISTORICAL MANUSCRIPTS COMMISSION *Seventeenth report* ... Cd.3737. H.M.S.O., 1907, 122-3.

RIGG, J.M. 'Muniments of the corporation of the city of Salisbury', in HISTORICAL MANUSCRIPTS COMMISSION *Report on manuscripts in various collections* **4**. Cd.3218. H.M.S.O., 1907, 191-254.

HASKINS, C. *The ancient trade guilds and companies of Salisbury*. Salisbury: Bennett Bros., 1912. Includes many extracts from original sources, giving names.

Infirmary
Salisbury 200: the bi-centenary of Salisbury Infirmary, 1766-1966. Salisbury: Salisbury General Hospital, 1967. Includes list of officers, 1766-1966.

St.Edmund
SWAYNE, HENRY JAMES FOWLE, ed. *Churchwardens accounts of S.Edmund & S.Thomas, Sarum, 1443-1702, with other documents*. Wilts Record Society [1]. Salisbury: Bennett Brothers, 1896.

St.Martin
BAKER, T.H. *Notes on St.Martin's church and parish*. Salisbury: Brown & Co., 1906. Salisbury; includes lists of incumbents, churchwardens, parish clerks, sextons and organists; extracts from churchwardens accounts, etc.

Trinity Hospital
BAKER, T.H. 'The Trinity Hospital, Salisbury', *W.A.M.* **36**(113), 1910, 376-412. Includes list of chaplains and subwardens, 15-18th c., rentals, 1638 and 1666, extracts from accounts, deeds, etc.

SMITH, WILLIAM. 'A medieval archive from Trinity Hospital, Salisbury', *Archives* **16**(69), 1983, 39-46. General discussion of almshouse records, mainly deeds, 13-19th c.

Savernake Forest
BRENTNALL, H.C. 'Venison trespasses in the reign of Henry VII', *W.A.M.* **53**(191), 1949, 191-212. Includes many presentments, with names, relating to Savernake Forest.

Administration continued

Savernake Forest continued

CARDIGAN, EARL OF. *The wardens of Savernake Forest*. Routledge & Kegan Paul, 1949. Originally published *W.A.M.* 51(184), 1946, 271-339; 51(186), 1947, 500-554; 52(188), 1948, 139-94; 53(190), 1949, 1-62. Primarily concerned with the Esturmy, Seymour, Bruce and Brudenall families, medieval-20th c. Includes pedigrees.

Seend

BRADBY, EDWARD. 'Seend contra Napoleon, 1798', *W.A.M.* 77, 1983, 109-21. Includes list of 63 contributors to fund for defence against Napoleon, with list of landowners and occupiers.
'The stoks of Seen' churche', *W.N.Q.* 2, 1896-8, 528-31 & 571-7. Medieval bede roll of Seend church, i.e. record of provision for lights, obits, etc., made by deceased parishioners. Includes brief pedigree of 15th c. Stokes family.

Steeple Ashton

KNUBLEY, E.P. 'Steeple Ashton churchwardens' accounts', *W.N.Q.* 6, 1908-10, 364-76, 420-8, 468-73, 518-23 & 567-70; 7, 1911-13, 34-9, 70-76, 138-42, 184-8, 224-8, 279-82, 329-31, 373-7, 469-73, 492-6 & 556-9. See also 8, 1914-16, 471. 16-17th c.

Stert

See Urchfont

Trowbridge

STOTE, A.W. 'Some notes on Trowbridge parish church registers', *W.A.M.* 42(138), 1923, 219-26. General discussion of parish records, including list of rate arrears, 1679.

Tytherton Lucas

SYMONDS, W. 'Memorandum book of Thomas Gardiner of Tytherton Lucas', *W.N.Q.* 7, 1911-13, 60-65, 100-105 & 147-52. Includes lists of ratepayers, 1680-93, tithing men, 1677-1749, and overseers, 1691-1747, with notes on local births, marriages and deaths, etc., especially of Gardiner family.

Urchfont

THOMPSON, E. MARGARET. 'Records of Wiltshire parishes: Erchfont with Stert', *W.N.Q.* 4, 1902-4, 295-304, 356-65, 393-403, 441-51, 494-9 & 544-51; 5, 1905-7, 9-16, 60-67, 104-17, 153-68, 199-211, 248-61, 295-301, 340-46, 396-403, 442-52, 486-94 & 544-9; 6, 1908-10, 10-19, 60-69, 114-21, 161-7 & 201-8. Medieval-19th c. deeds, inquisitions post mortem, subsidies, manorial accounts and court rolls, wills, etc.

Wilton

'Wilton Corporation charters', *Journal of the British Archaeological Association* 17, 1861, 311-18. Includes medieval deeds, etc., with will of John Fromond, 1348.

Winterslow

SYMONDS, W. 'Winterslow church reckonings, 1542-1661', *W.A.M.* 36(111), 1909, 27-49. Extracts from churchwardens' accounts, with list of churchwardens.

Wootton Bassett

'Petition to Parliament from the borough of Wotton Basset, in the reign of Charles I, relative to the right of the burgesses to free common of pasture in Fasterne Great Park', *Topographer & genealogist* 3, 1858, 22-5. Gives names of petitioners.

16. EDUCATION

The records of schools can provide the genealogist with much useful information. For the history of Wiltshire schools in the medieval period, see:

ORME, NICHOLAS. *Education in the West of England, 1066-1548: Cornwall, Devon, Dorset, Gloucestershire, Wiltshire.* Exeter: University of Exeter, 1976.

There are a number of histories of individual schools, and a few school registers have also been published, as has the diary of an 18th c. schoolmaster. School histories usually list headmasters; they may also include the names of assistant teachers and/or pupils. Some, of course, have much greater genealogical value than others. The following list is not comprehensive; rather, it includes only those works which mention many names.

Bratton

REEVES, MARJORIE, & MORRISON, JEAN, eds. *The diaries of Jeffery Whitaker, schoolmaster of Bratton, 1739-1741.* W.R.S. **44**, 1989. Includes notes on his family, and on other families and individuals mentioned.

Chippenham

PLATTS, ARNOLD. *Chippenham Grammar School, 1896-1956: a history of the school.* Chippenham: the School, 1956. Includes many names of staff and pupils.

Godolphin School

DOUGLAS, M.A., & ASH, C.R., eds. *The Godolphin School, 1726-1926.* Longmans, 1928. Includes will of Elizabeth Godolphin, 1726, pedigree of Godolphin, lists of trustees, staff, head girls, etc.

Marlborough

JAMES, L. WARWICK. *Marlborough College register, 1843-1952, with alphabetical index.* 9th ed. Marlborough: the College, 1952.

STEDMAN, A.R. 'A history of Marlborough Grammar School', *W.A.M.* **51**(182), 1945, 41-112. Includes pedigrees of Foster, Merriman, and others associated with the school.

Salisbury

HAPPOLD, F.C. *Bishop Wordsworth's School, 1890-1950.* Salisbury: the School, 1950. Includes lists of scholarship winners and war deaths, etc.

STANTON, W.K. *A register of the Chorister's School, Salisbury, 1810-1921.* 2nd ed. Green & Co., 1921.

WORDSWORTH, CHRISTOPHER. 'Salisbury choristers: their endowments, boy-bishops, music teachers, and head-masters, with the history of the organ', *W.A.M.* **47**(168), 1938, 201-31. Includes many names, with deed abstracts.

Warminster

HOPE, ROBERT. *Warminster School: the Lord Weymouth School register, 1707-1895.* [Warminster]: Old Verlucians Society, 1972. Includes lists of both staff and students, with biographical notes.

17. EMIGRATION

Many Wiltshire men and women emigrated to North America, South Africa, Australia and New Zealand, where their descendants often take a lively interest in their origins. It is not the purpose here to provide a full listing of everything published on Wiltshire emigrants, but rather to identify a few readily available works which may be useful. Further assistance may be had by consulting the works listed in section 16 of *English textgenealogy: an introductory bibliography*. A brief general discussion of sources for migration to Australia and Canada in the mid-19th c. is provided by:

GIBSON, J.S.W. 'Assisted emigration of paupers from Wiltshire, 1834-1847', *W.F.H.S.* **7**, 1982, 18-19.

Australia

A valuable general introduction is provided by:

BROWN, MARTYN. *Australia bound! The story of West Country connections, 1688-1888.* Bradford on Avon: Ex Libris Press, 1988. See also:

CASWELL, VERONICA. *The Wiltshire Emigration Association, 1849-1851: index to persons who applied to emigrate to Australia (including 195 who did not go).* Wiltshire Family History Society, 1987.

SMITH, MARTIN. 'Wiltshire convicts to Australia', *W.F.H.S.* **21**, 1986, 25-6. Includes brief list, 1788-1817.

SMITH, MARTIN. 'The deserters', *W.F.H.S.* **21**, 1986, 27-8. Wiltshire deserters in Australia, early 19th c., includes list.

Canada

PRONG, DONNA-REA. 'Migrants to Canada: passengers from Wiltshire who were cleared by the Montreal Emigration Society on their arrival in Upper Canada from 12th May to 5th November, 1832', *W.F.H.S.* **40**, 1991, 10. List.

New Zealand

SMITH, GRACE M. 'Some emigrants from Wiltshire to Canterbury, New Zealand, 1850-1879', *W.F.H.S.* **3**, 1981, 18. Lists arrivals at the port of Lyttelton.

South Africa

WILLIAMS, J. ROBERT. 'Wiltshire settlers in South Africa, 1820', *W.F.H.S.* **7**, 1983, 4-7. Includes many names.

HADDON, GORDON WM. 'Emigration to South Africa', *W.F.H.S.* **39**, 1990, 12-13. Includes list of Wiltshire emigrants, 1820.

United States

COLDHAM, PETER WILSON. *Bonded passengers to America, volume V: Western Circuit, 1664-1775, comprising the counties of Cornwall, Devon, Dorset, Hampshire, Somerset and Wiltshire, with a list of the rebels of 1685.* Baltimore: Genealogical Publishing, 1983. Lists transported convicts.

HOMER-WOOFF, GERALD. 'Emigrants to New England', *W.F.H.S.* **36**, 1990, 36. From Wiltshire, 1620-50: list.

GODDARD, JULIE. 'Are they in Utah?', *W.F.H.S.* **10**, 1983, 21-2. Discussion of Mormon emigrants to Utah, 19th c., with notes on Haskell family.

SALERNO, A. 'The social background of seventeenth-century emigration to America', *Journal of British Studies* **19**(1), 1979, 31-52. Study of 81 Wiltshire emigrants; gives many useful bibliographical references.

FAMILY NAME INDEX

PLACE NAME INDEX

AUTHOR INDEX